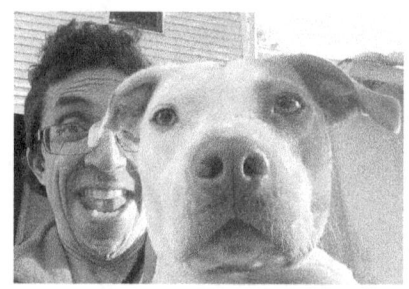

David Gerbstadt and his dog NOEL.

It was his first year in college where a professor saw something and strongly suggested that he become an art major. David declared his major and shortly after that said a vow, 'through rich or poor sickness and health no matter what I will make art!' From then on the ideas kept coming. David had found what he loved to do.... art. Often times he would be working til 3 am at the art building or in his room. Eating in his studio clothes at the dining hall was a regular thing. He simply lived, breathed, and drank art. David Graduated from Millersville University in 1992.

After college, David decided early on to show anywhere and everywhere. He would load up dozens of paintings each weekend and head off to a new spot. Sometimes it was a tiny church flea market which had the best ribs or a huge art festival over a couple days.

From there David focused on selling his art in the streets at First Friday in Old City Philadelphia. In the beginning there were less than a half dozen artists doing this. An underground following grew.

David left art at street corners, train stations, all over his home town, New York City, San Francisco, Mexico, Austria, Poland. In all over 5,000 works were left for the taking. The size ranged from 7 feet high to about 3 inches. A film crew in 2000 produced the documentary film 'David was here' which can now be seen online about David leaving his art out for the taking. The film won an award at the Iowa international film festival. After that David stopped leaving his works out for the taking.

David's art is now in over 18 countries.

When asked, "What does his art mean?" David says, "I let the art I create speak for itself. I simply make it and put it into the world." A firm believer of "just do the work" in doing so you are free and the universe opens before you.

On December 28, 2007 just two days before flying home David died in route to the hospital in an ambulance after being run over by a tracker trailer truck. He was riding his bicycle at the time of the accident.

When the EMT'S got to David he had no pulse and was nearly out of blood. David never gave up though and an EMT named Jr. performed CPR in route to the waiting helicopter and brought David back to us. The next 9 hours David's heart stopped 4 more times and went through 40 units of blood and spent 2 months in the hospital.

The doctors all said he should be dead and asked him why is he still here? Yet, David lives on! His story of never giving up and take life one breath at a time is a lesson for us all.

Books available by David Gerbstadt on Amazon.com

"One Breath At a Time"

"The Red Heart Book"

"Bananas in Milk"

"Coloring Book"

David is a full time artist, author, and motivational speaker.

David says simply... "The truck did not stop him it just slowed him down..."
"Art healed me and continues to heal me..." I cope the best I can with PTSD.
"In the hospital I learned... that I am truly loved, I matter and worth it in this world to create art and to continue on..."

David Gerbstadt lives in Berwyn, Pa. with his 3 legged female pit mix 'Noel'.

Visit David on face book at: www.facebook.com/david.gerbstadt

ISBN 978-0-9849606-2-0

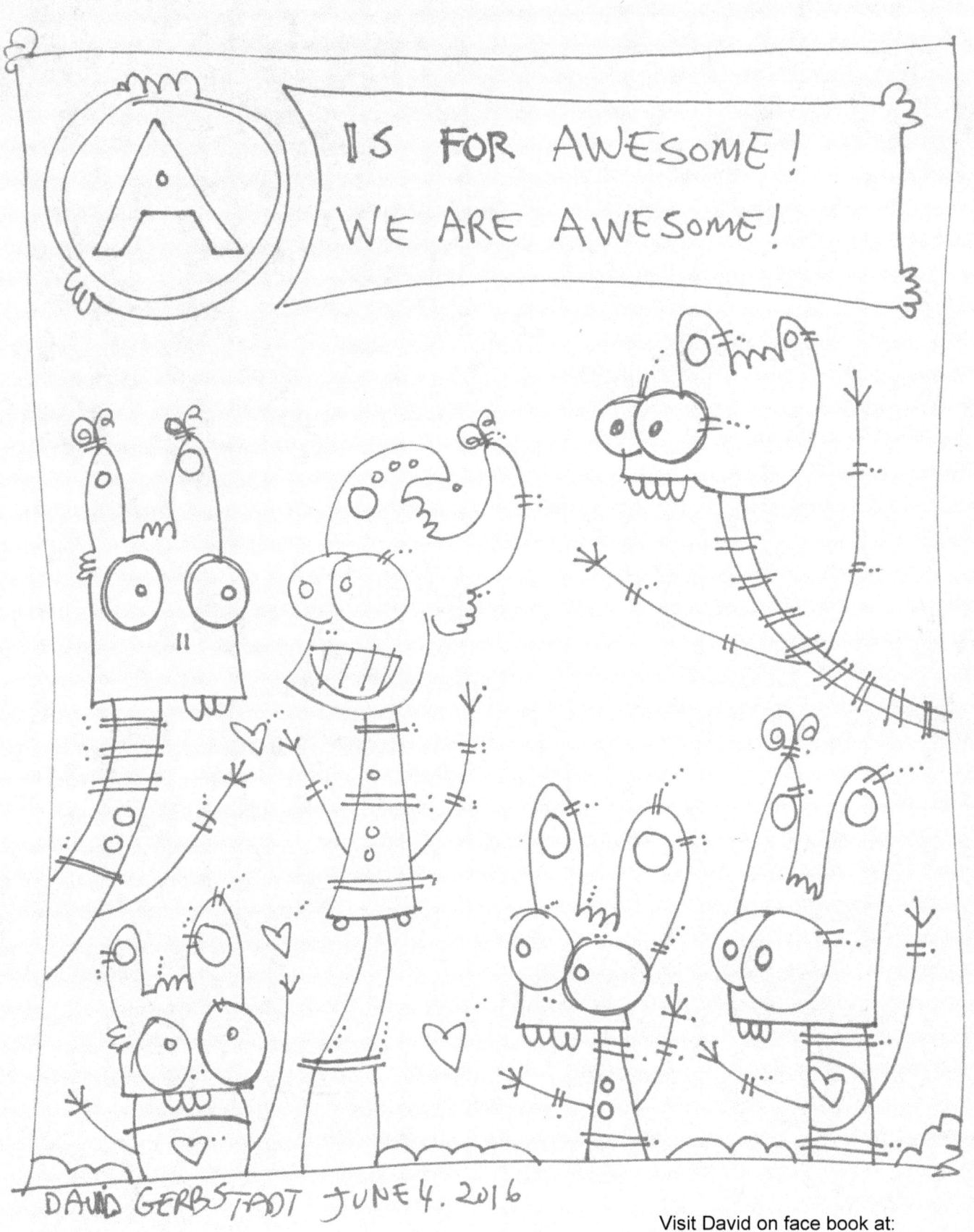

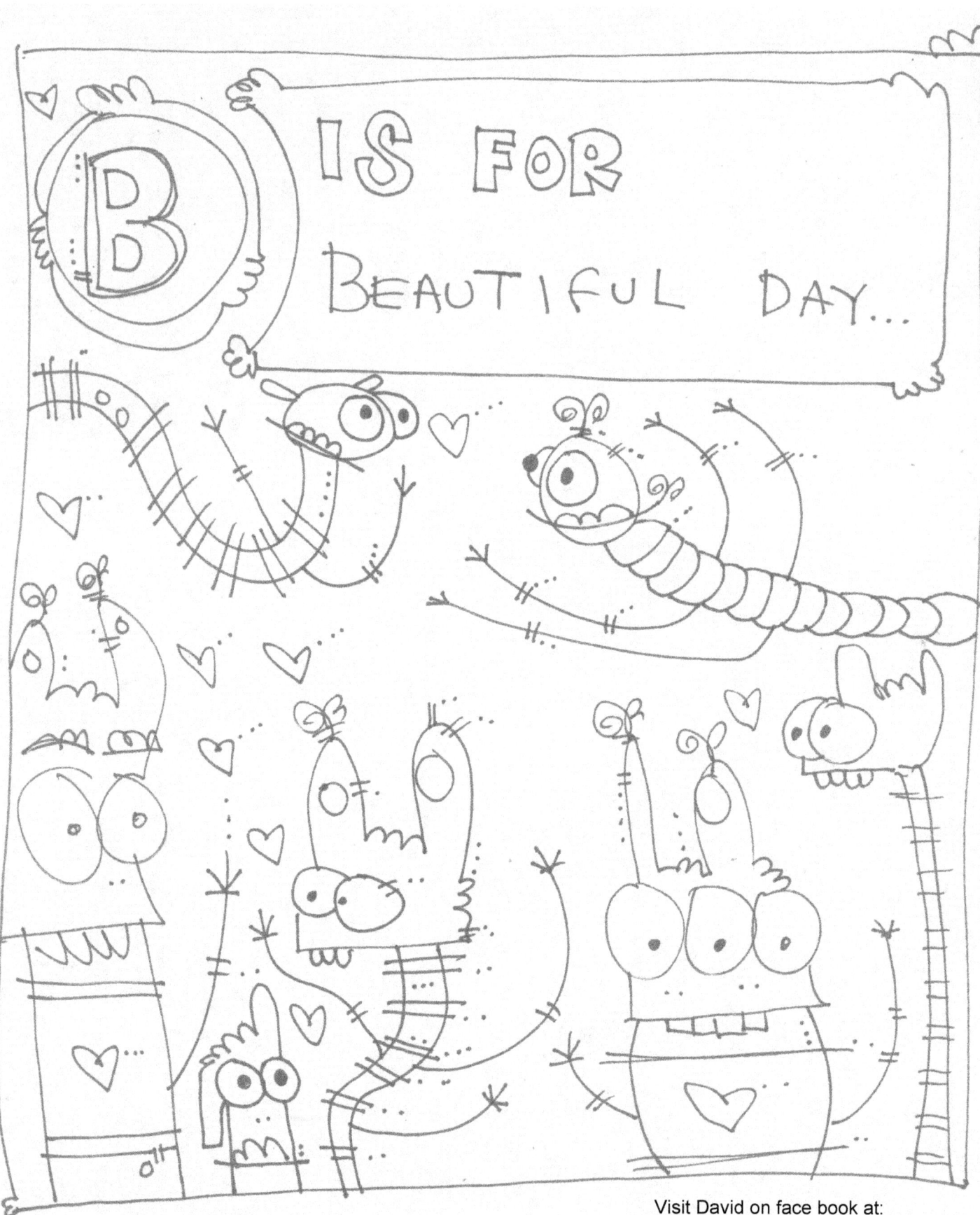

B IS FOR BEAUTIFUL DAY...

DAVID GERBSTADT JUNE 4, 2016...

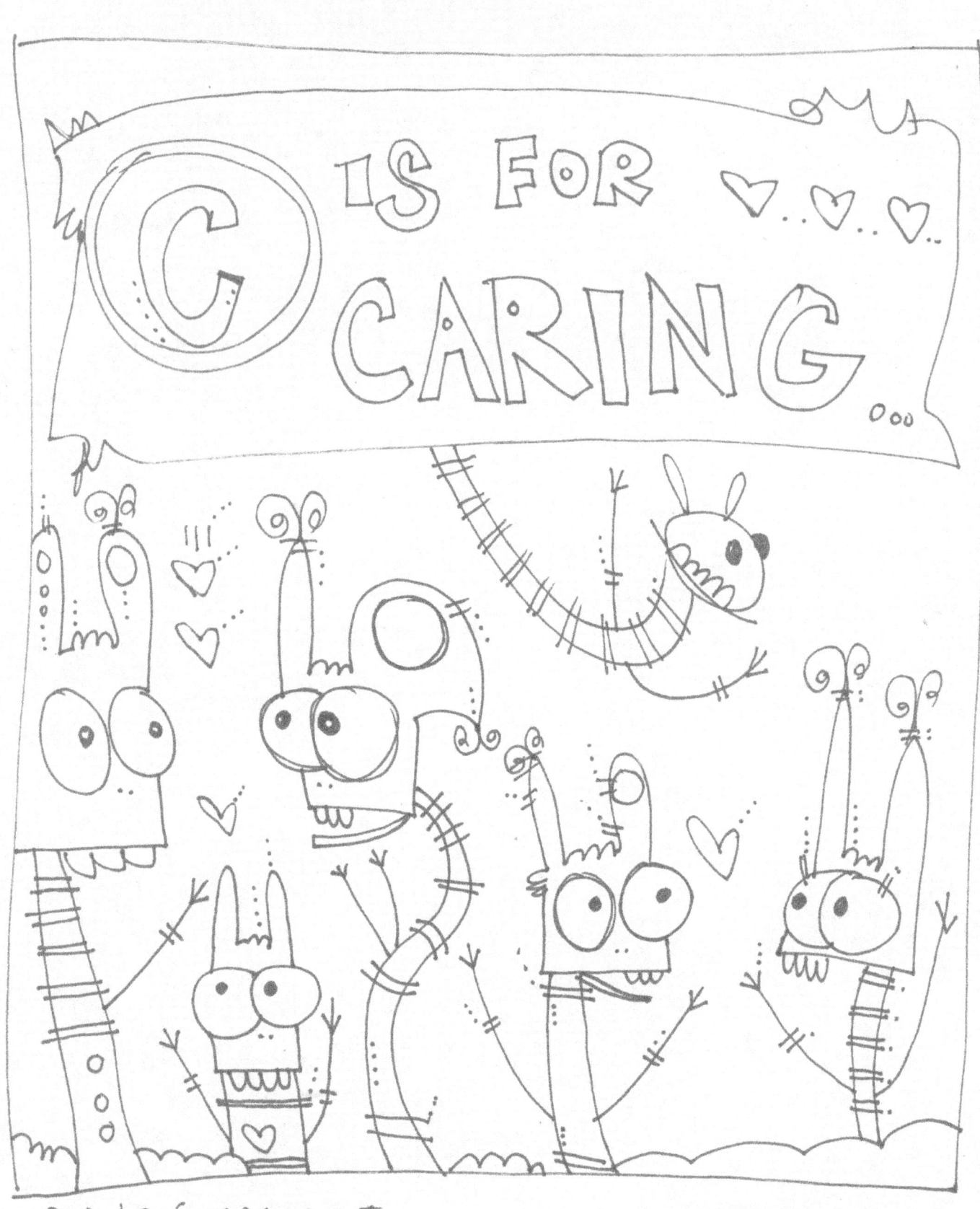

DAVID GERBSTADT JUNE 4. 2016

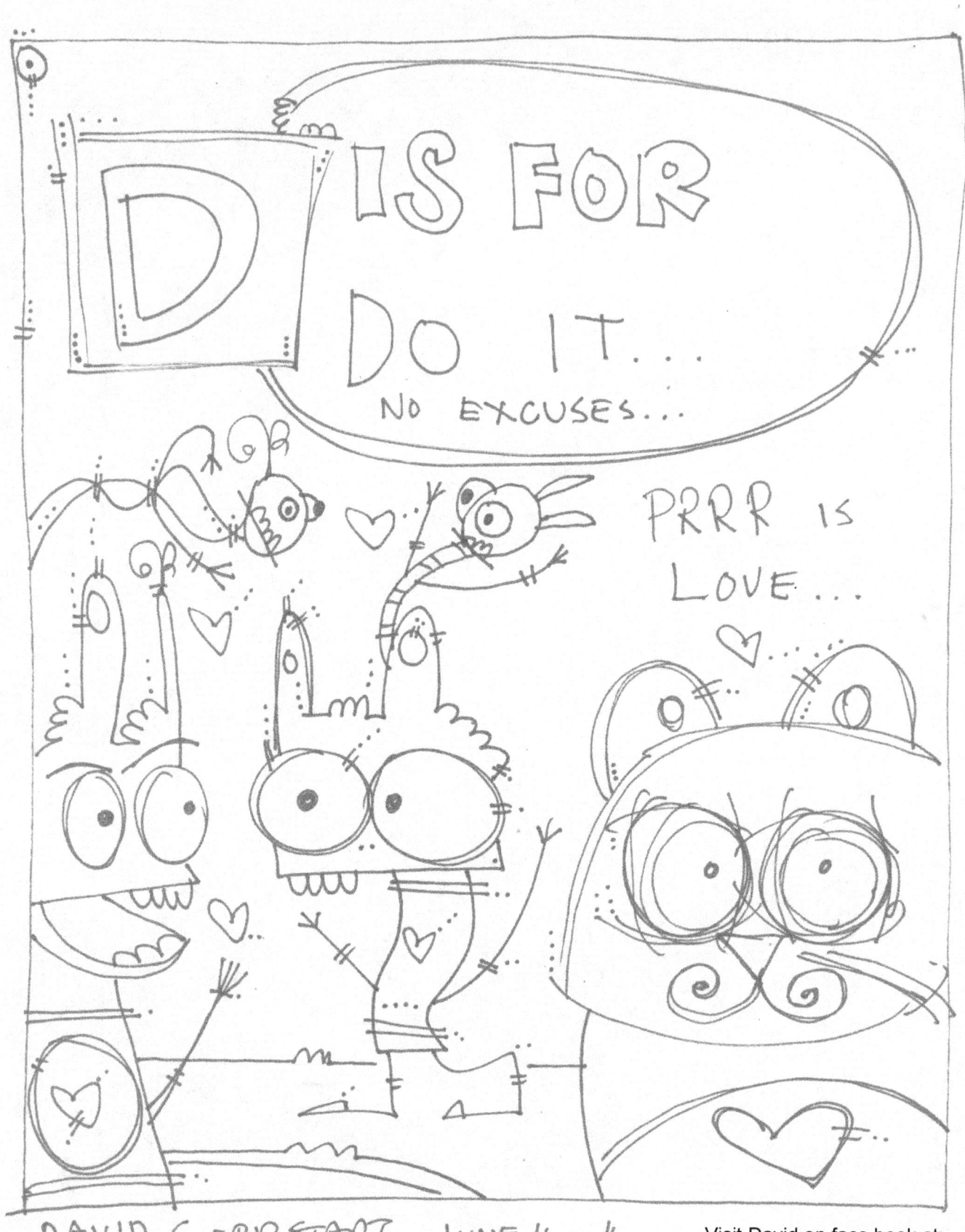

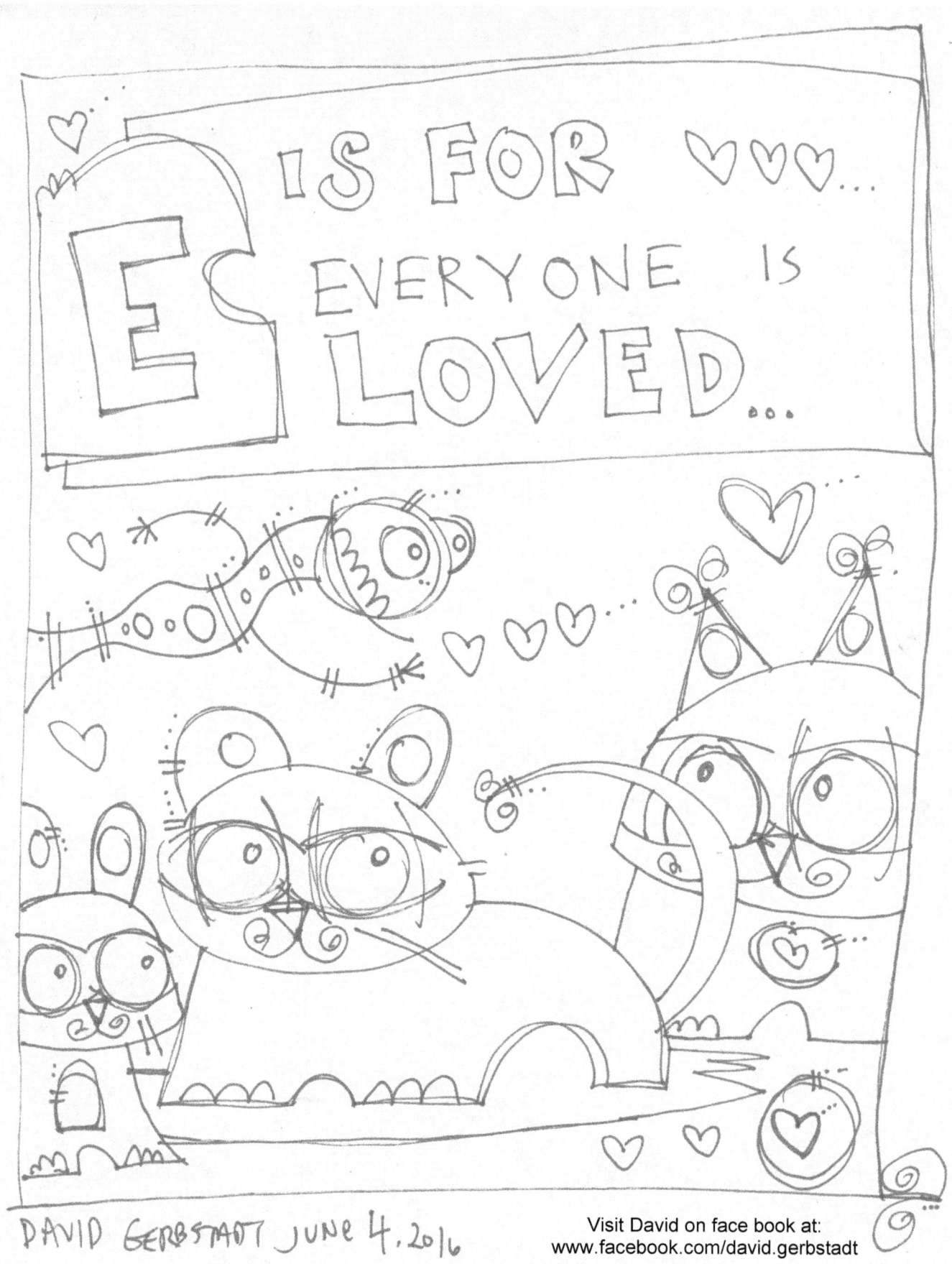

E IS FOR ♥ ♥♥...
EVERYONE IS LOVED...

DAVID GERBSTADT JUNE 4, 2016

Visit David on face book at:
www.facebook.com/david.gerbstadt

Coloring book and more books by
David Gerbstadt on Amazon.com

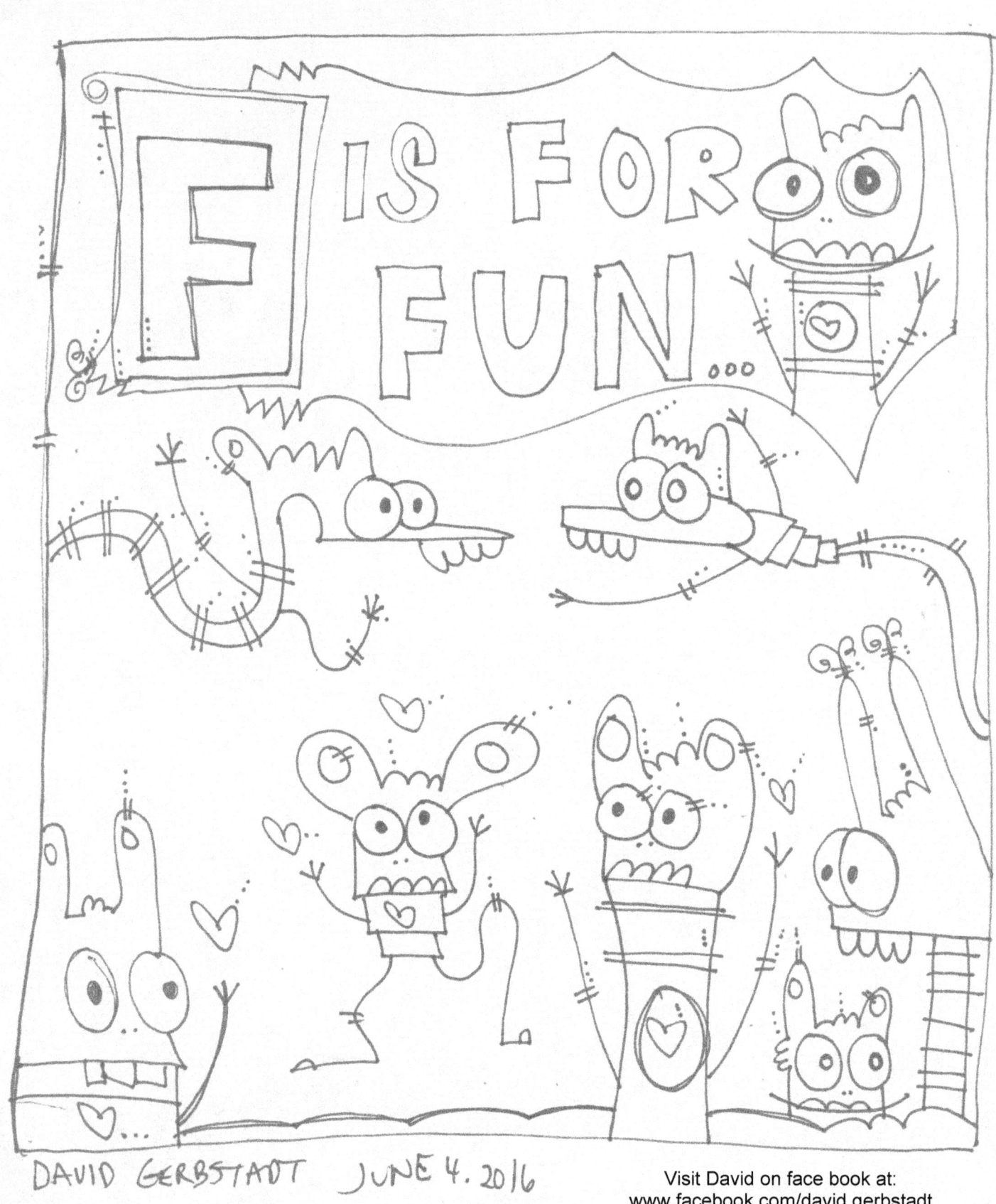

DAVID GERBSTADT JUNE 4. 2016

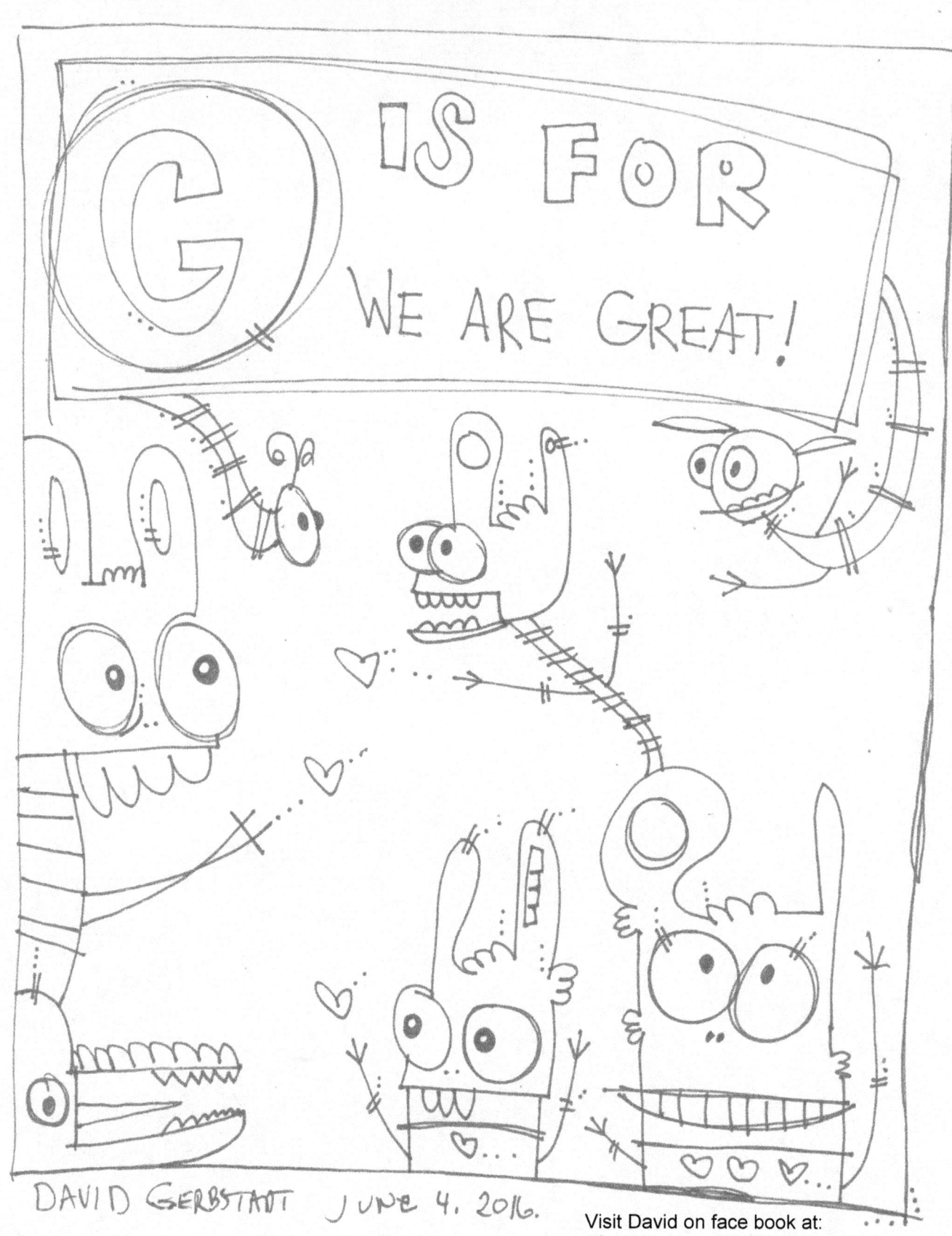

G IS FOR
WE ARE GREAT!

DAVID GERBSTADT   JUNE 4, 2016.

Visit David on face book at:
www.facebook.com/david.gerbstadt

Coloring book and more books by
David Gerbstadt on Amazon.com

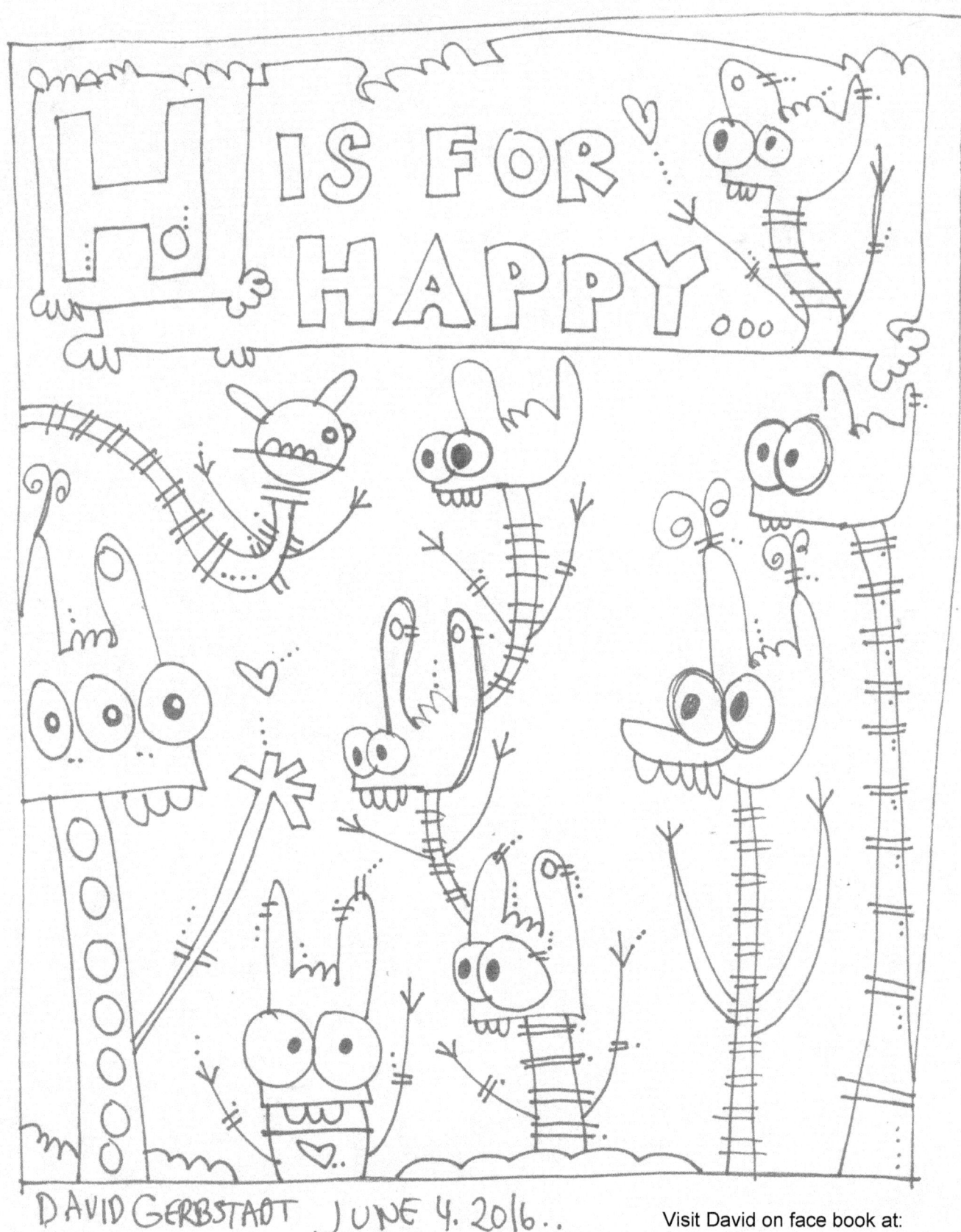

DAVID GERBSTADT JUNE 4. 2016..

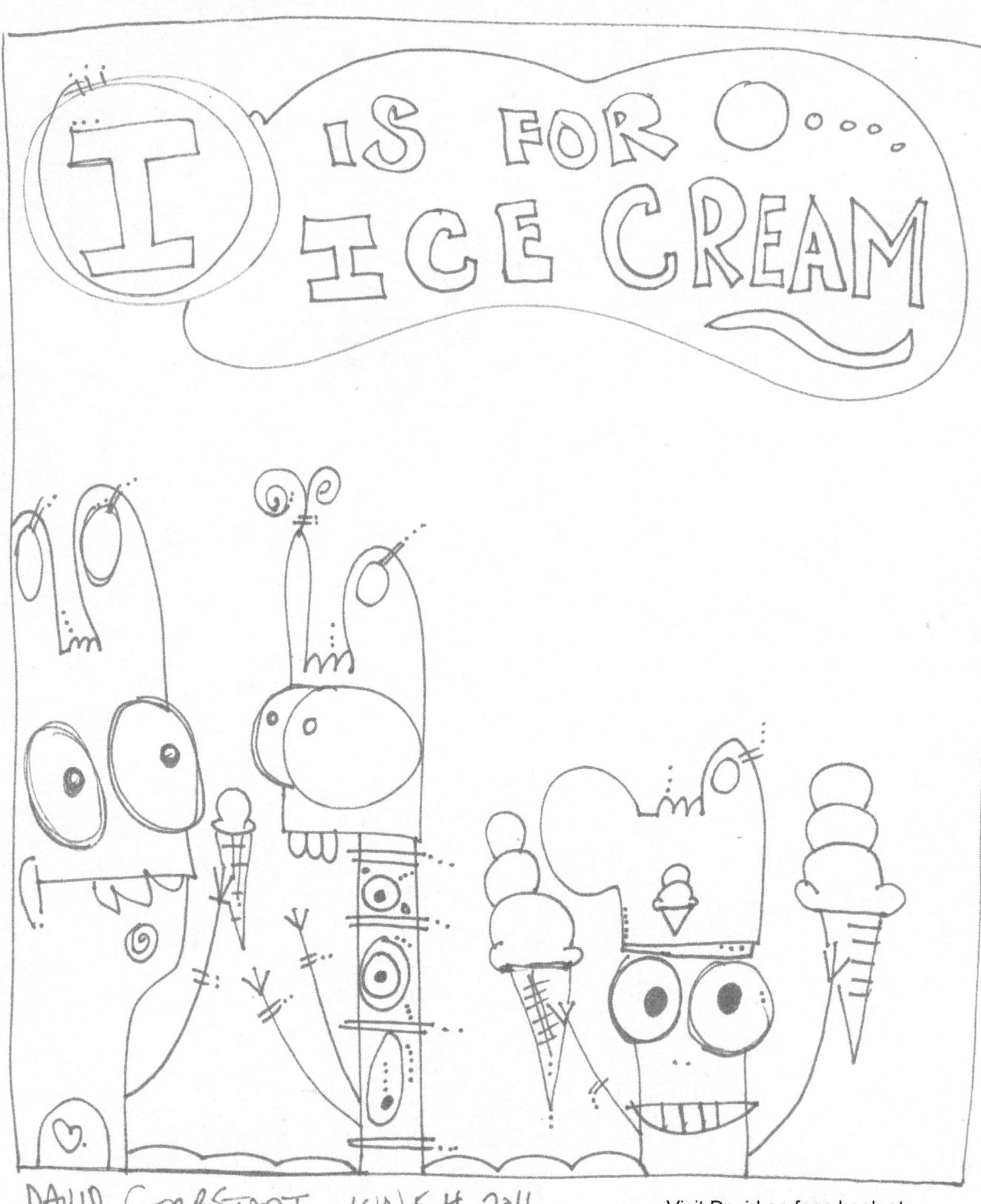

DAVID GERBSTADT JUNE 4, 2016

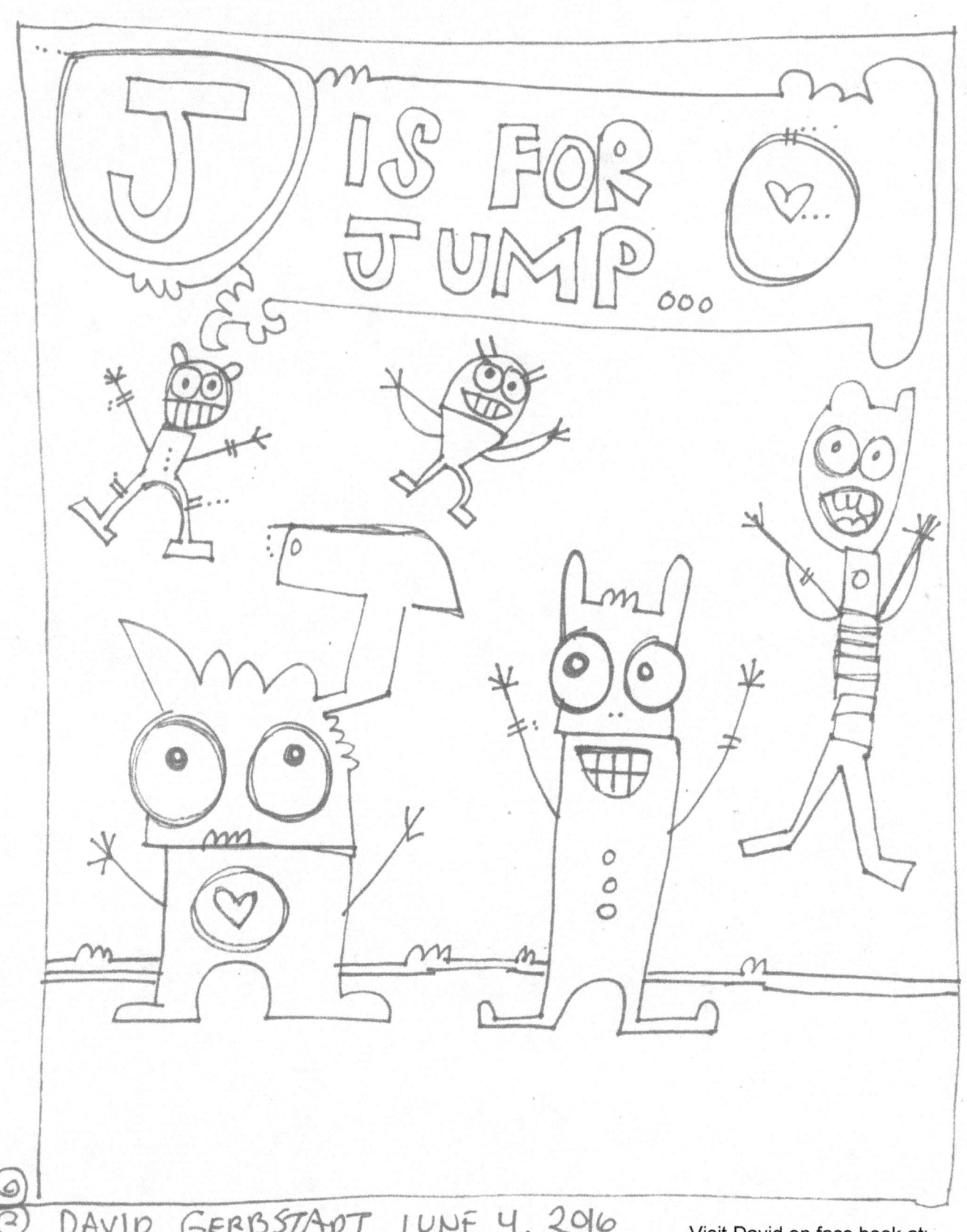

DAVID GERBSTADT JUNE 4, 2016

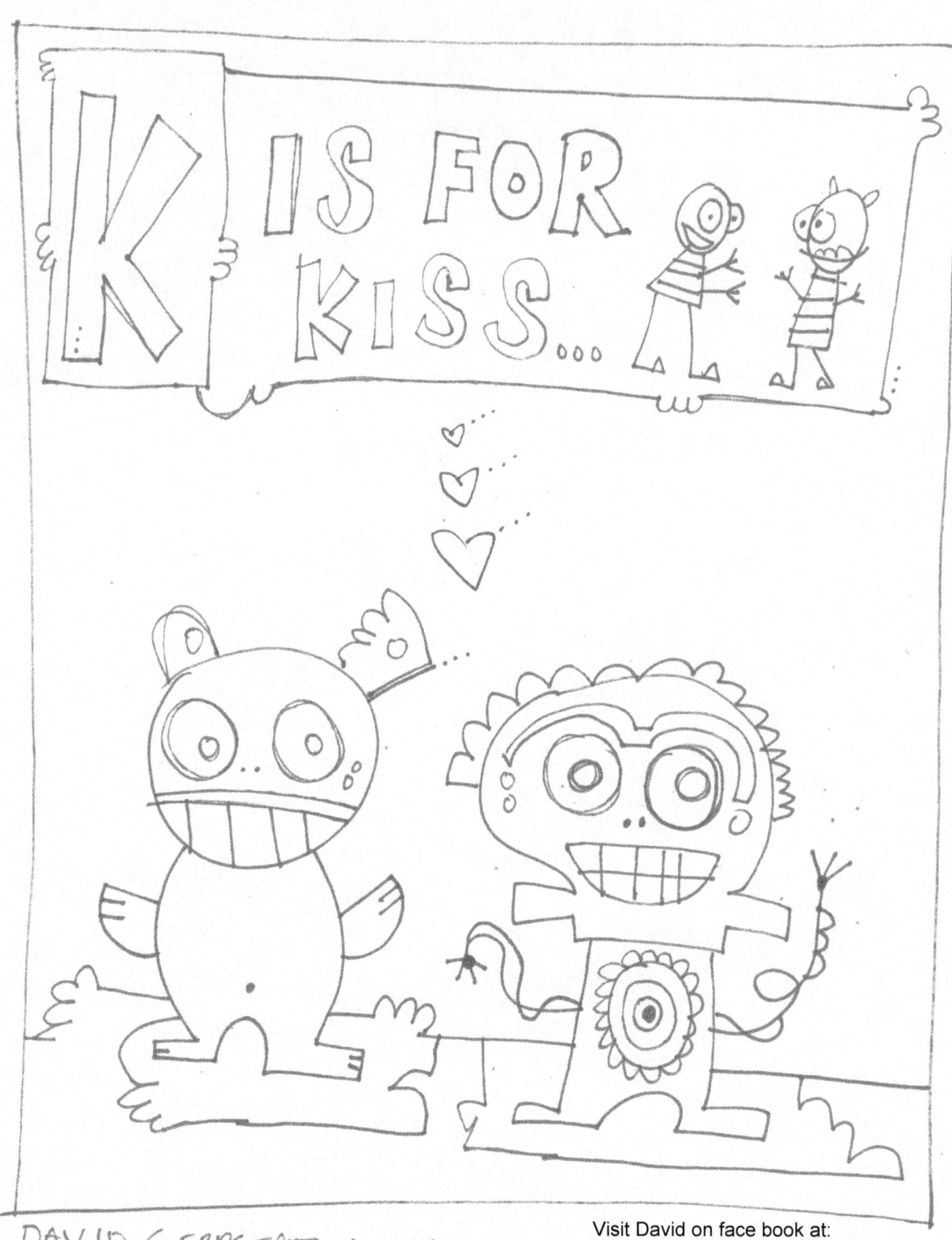

DAVID GERBSTADT JUNE 4.2016

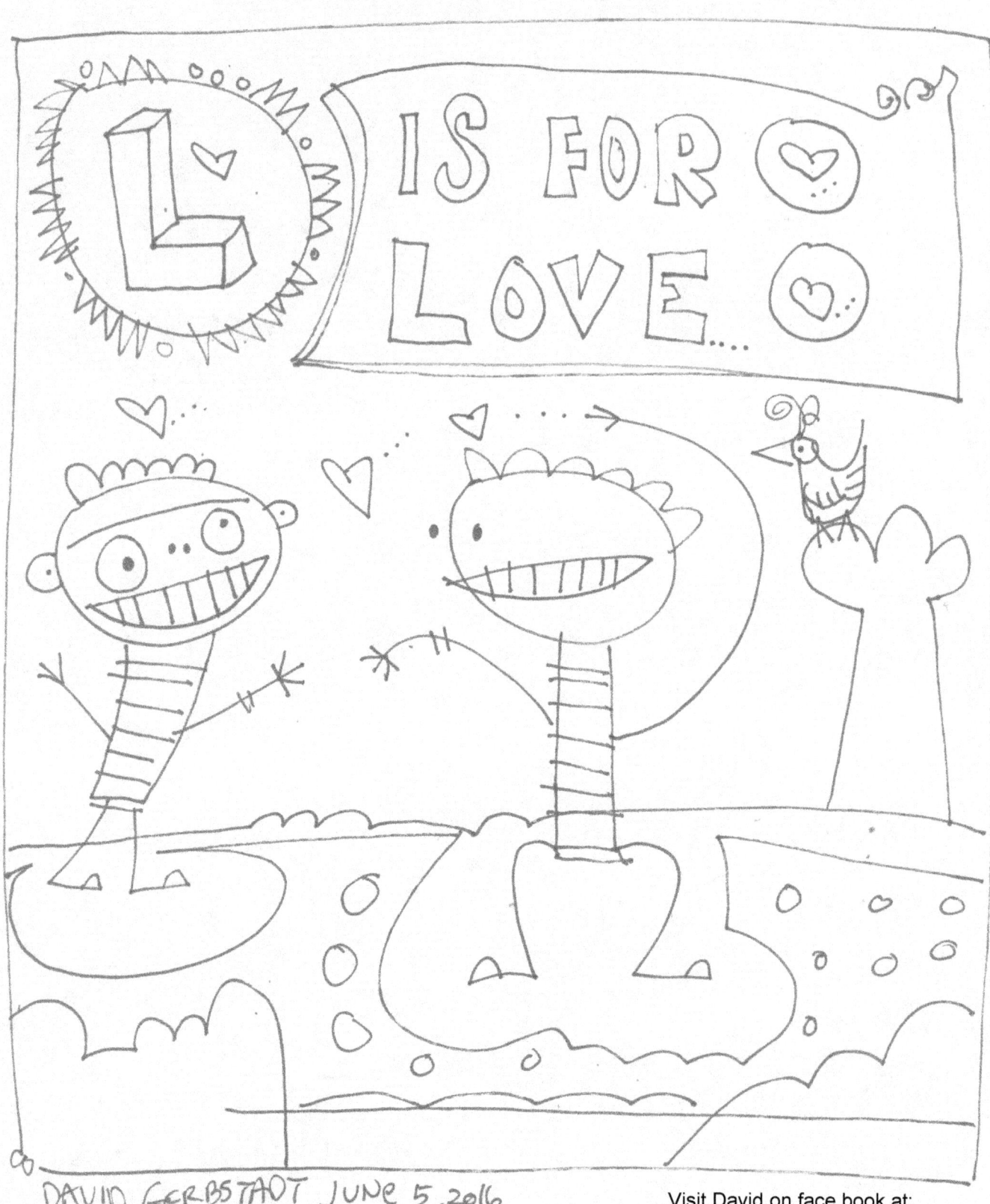

DAVID GERBSTADT JUNE 5. 2016

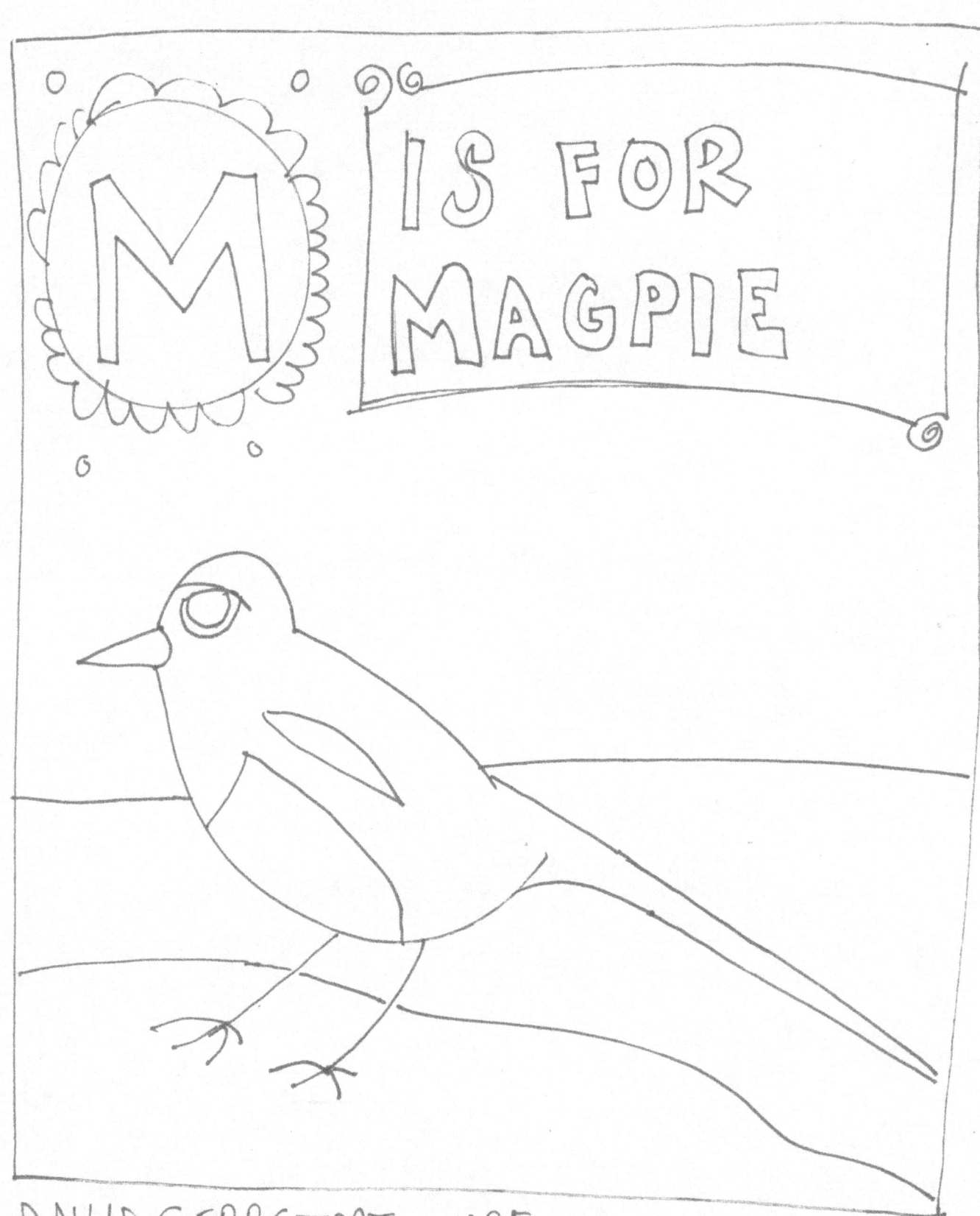

M IS FOR MAGPIE

DAVID GERBSTADT JUNE 5, 2016

Visit David on face book at:
www.facebook.com/david.gerbstadt

Coloring book and more books by
David Gerbstadt on Amazon.com

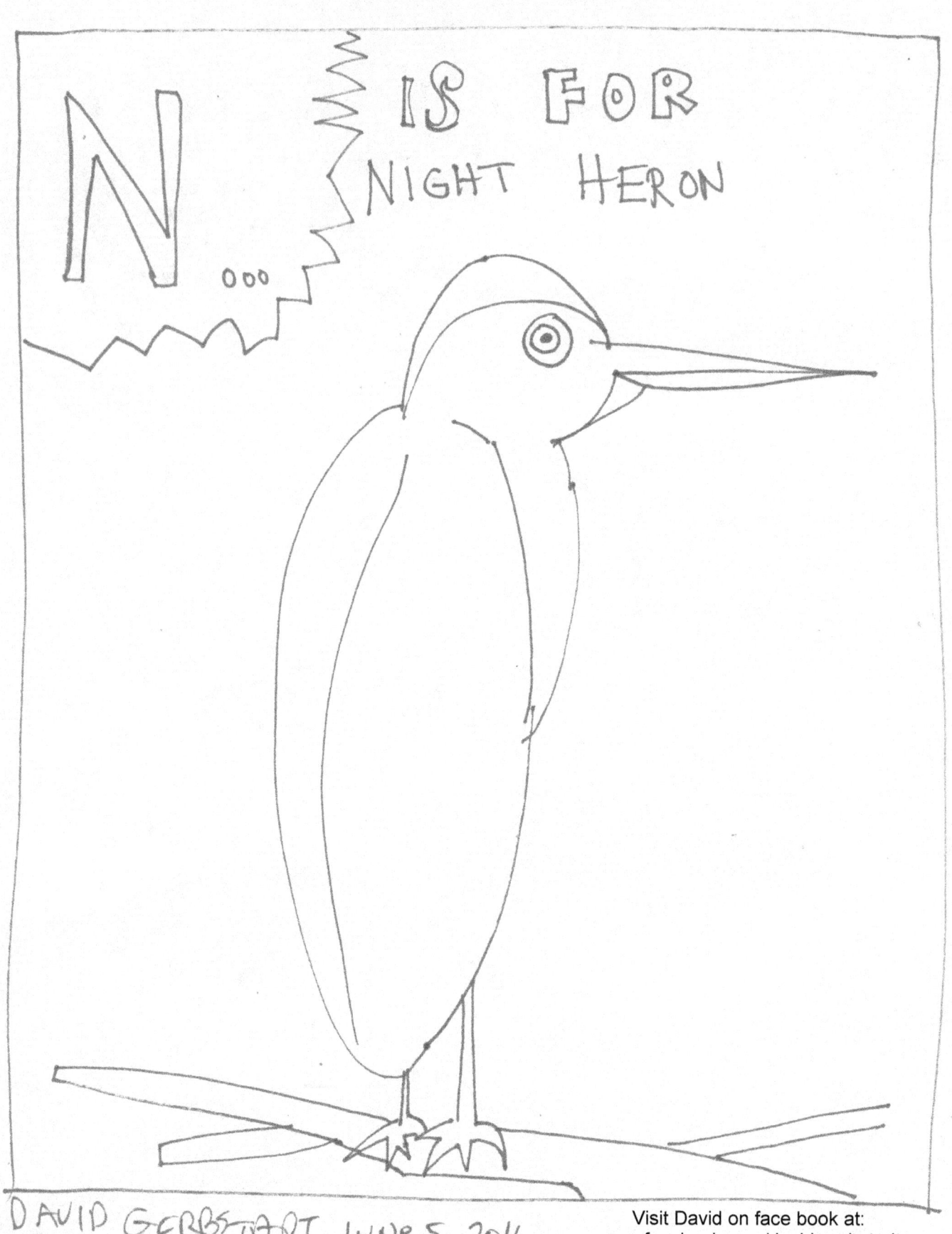

N... IS FOR NIGHT HERON

DAVID GERBSTADT JUNE 5, 2016.

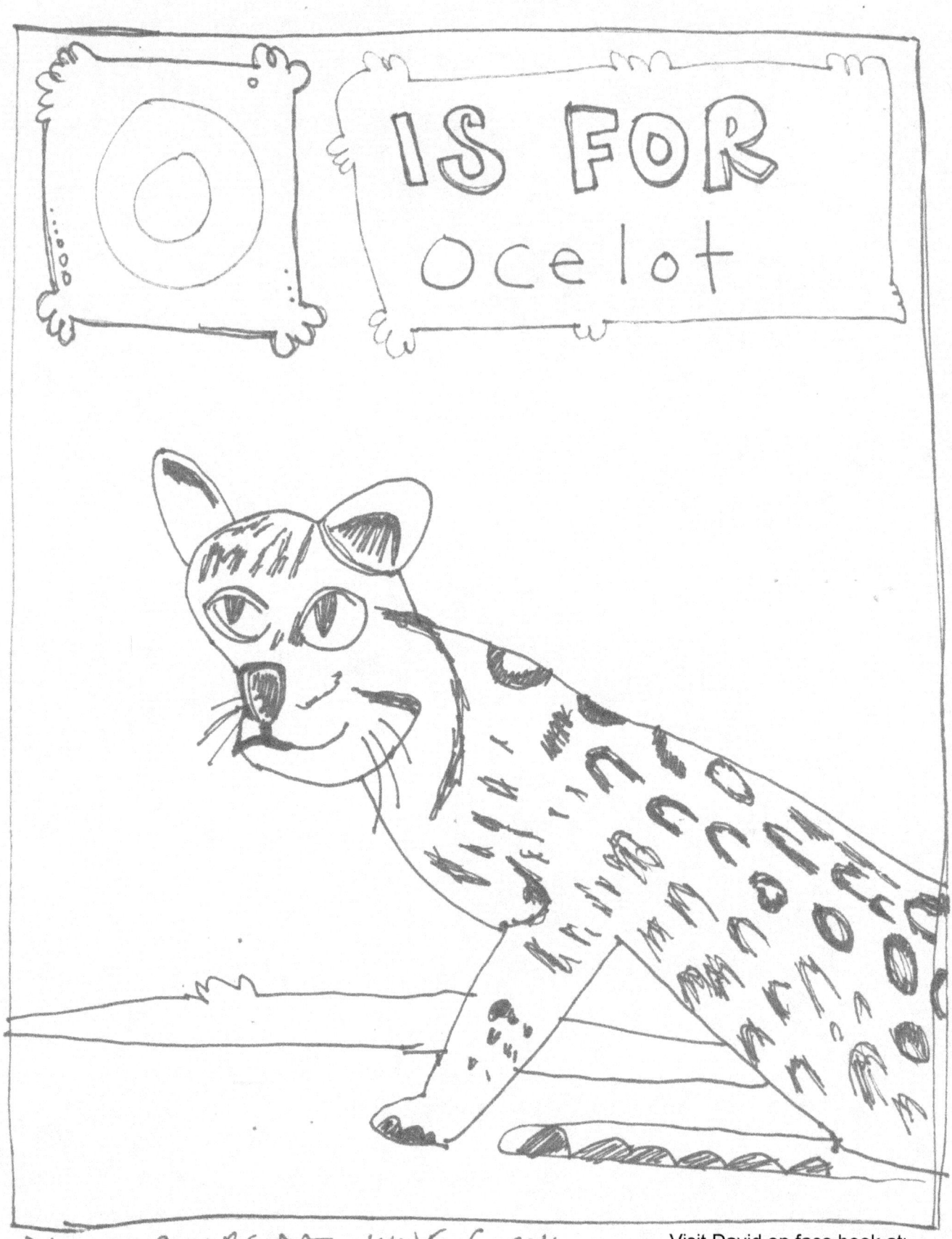

O IS FOR Ocelot

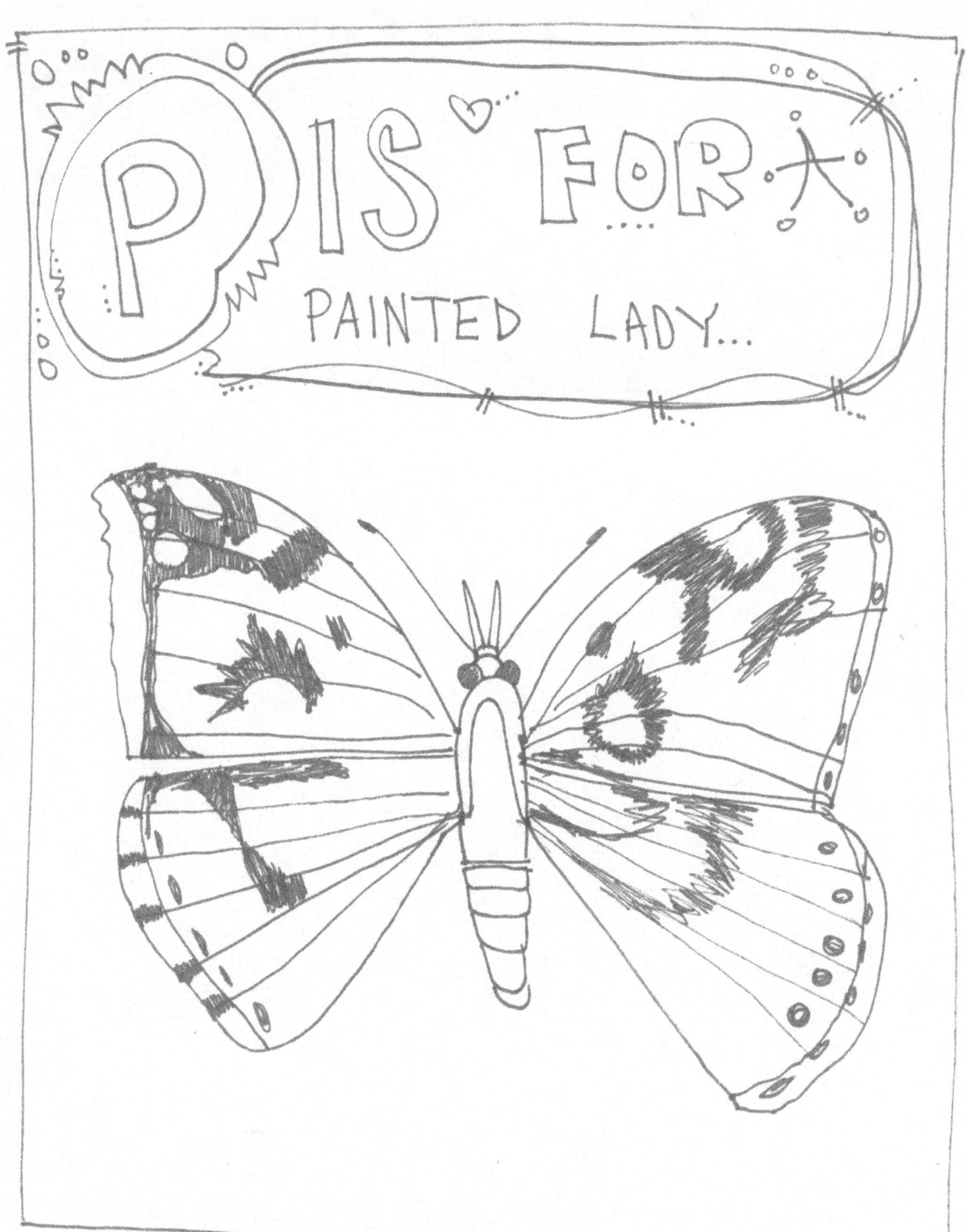

P IS FOR...

PAINTED LADY...

DAVID GERBSTADT JUNE 6, 2016...

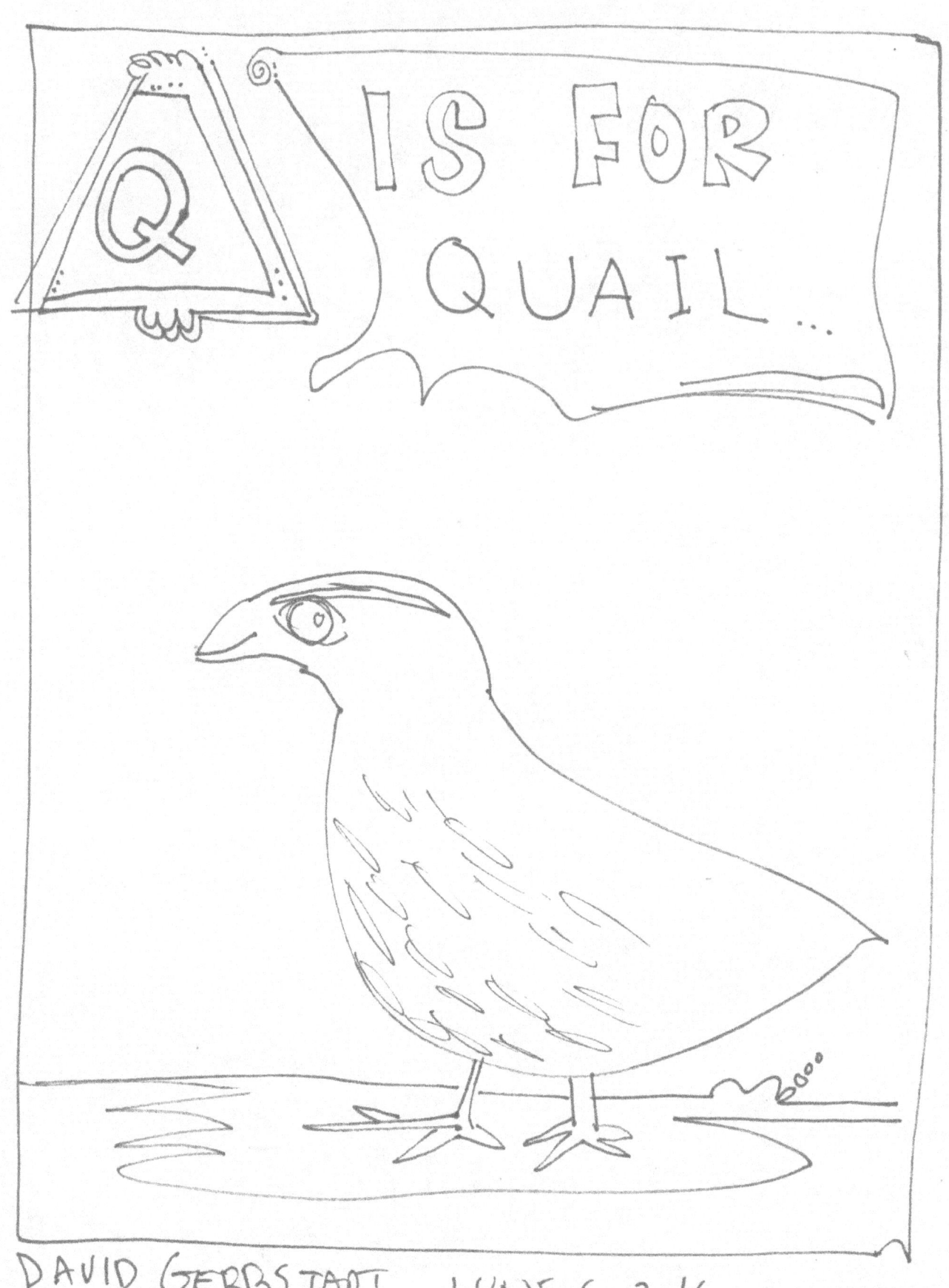

DAVID GERBSTADT   JUNE 6, 2016...

Visit David on face book at:
www.facebook.com/david.gerbstadt

Coloring book and more books by
David Gerbstadt on Amazon.com

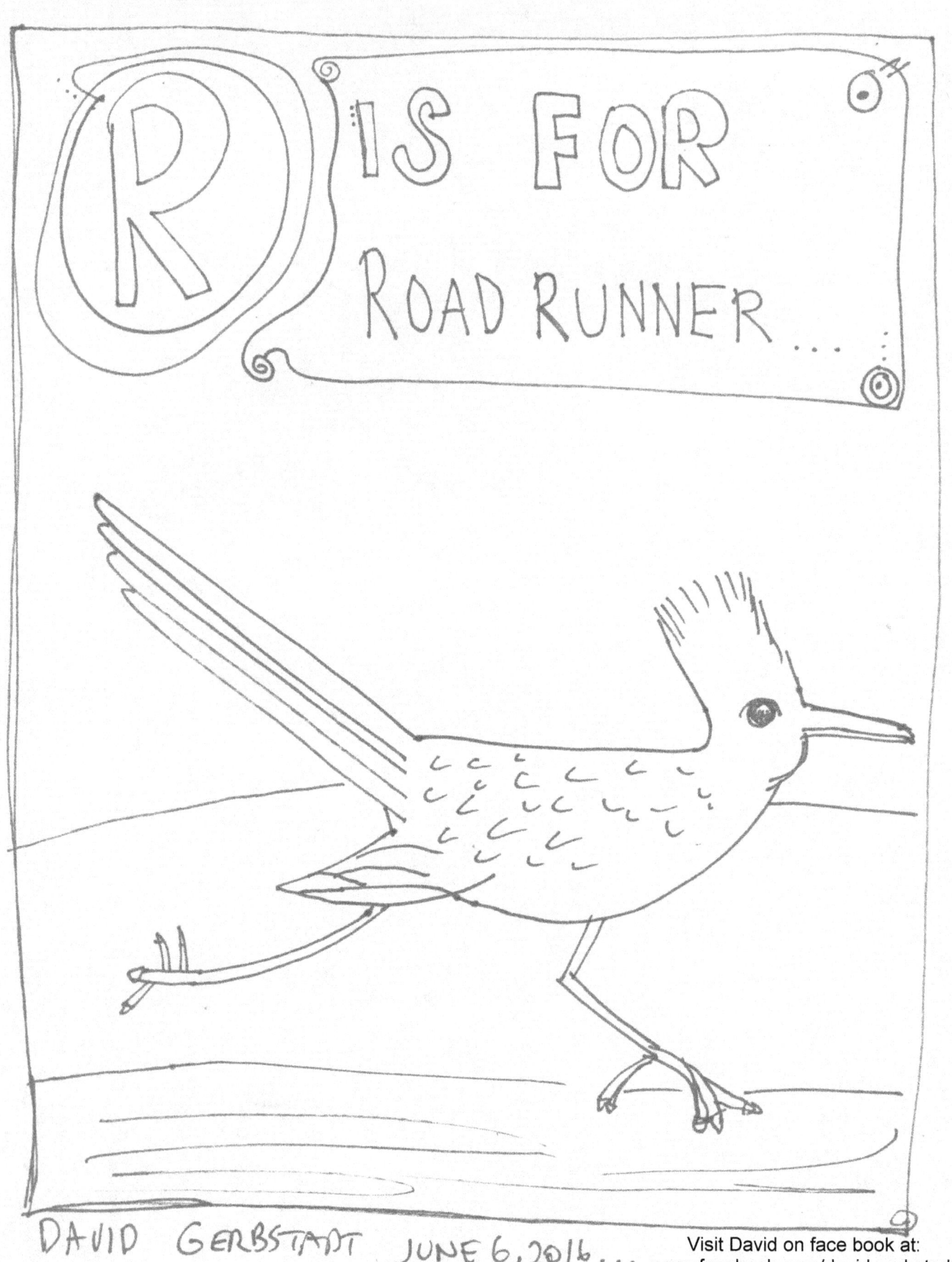

R IS FOR ROAD RUNNER...

DAVID GERBSTADT JUNE 6, 2016...

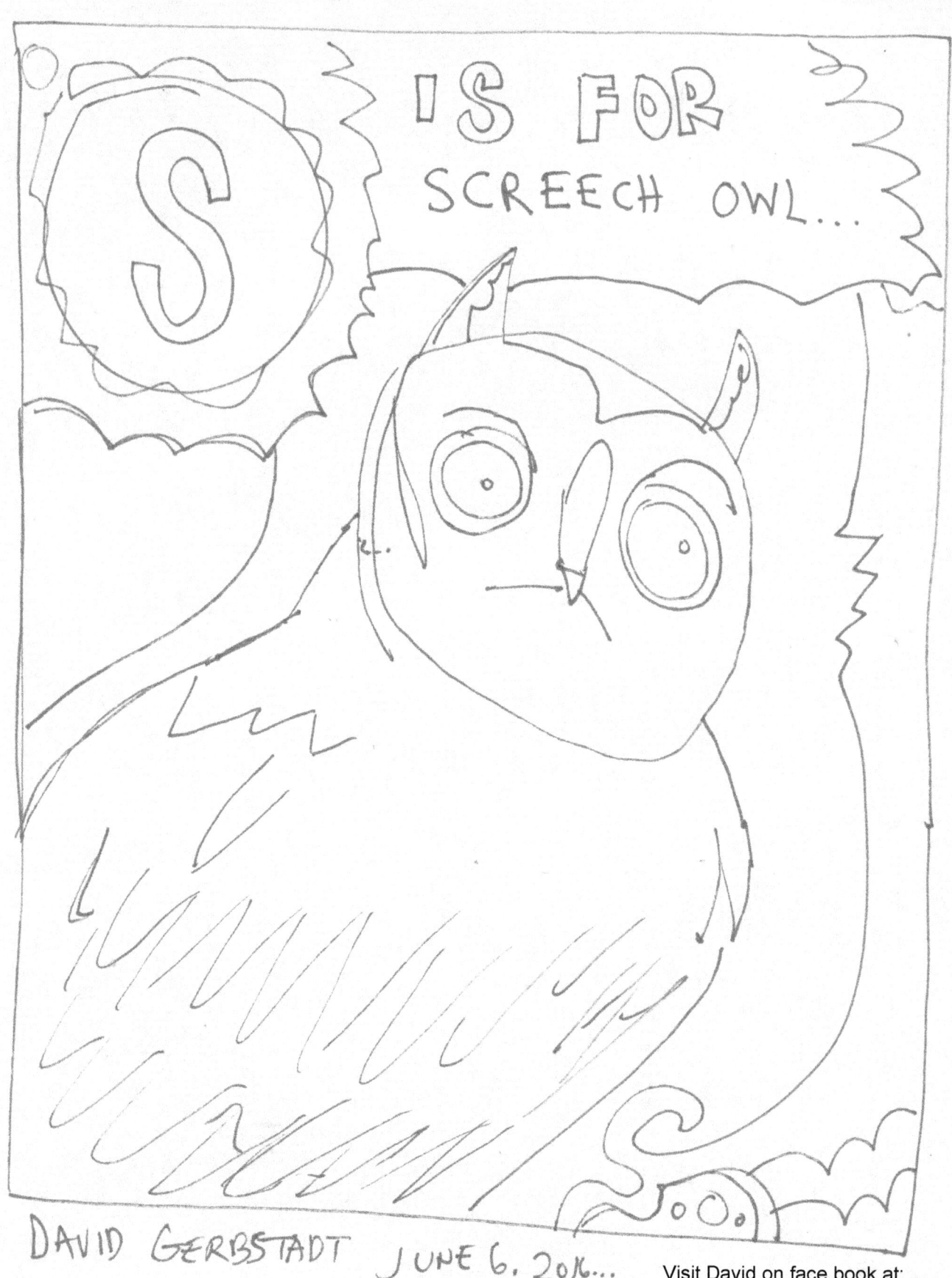

S IS FOR SCREECH OWL...

DAVID GERBSTADT JUNE 6, 2016...

Visit David on face book at:
www.facebook.com/david.gerbstadt

Coloring book and more books by
David Gerbstadt on Amazon.com

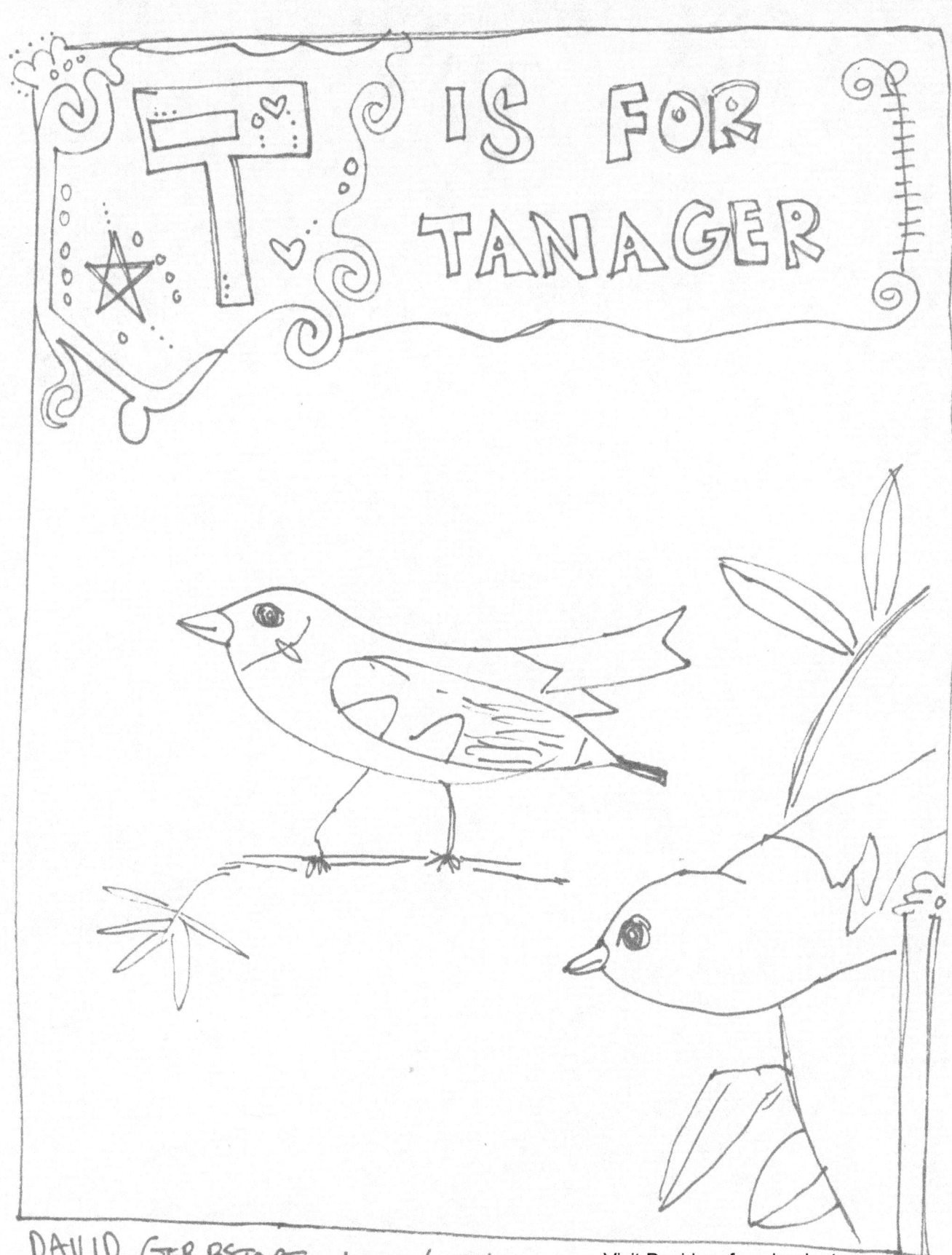

T IS FOR TANAGER

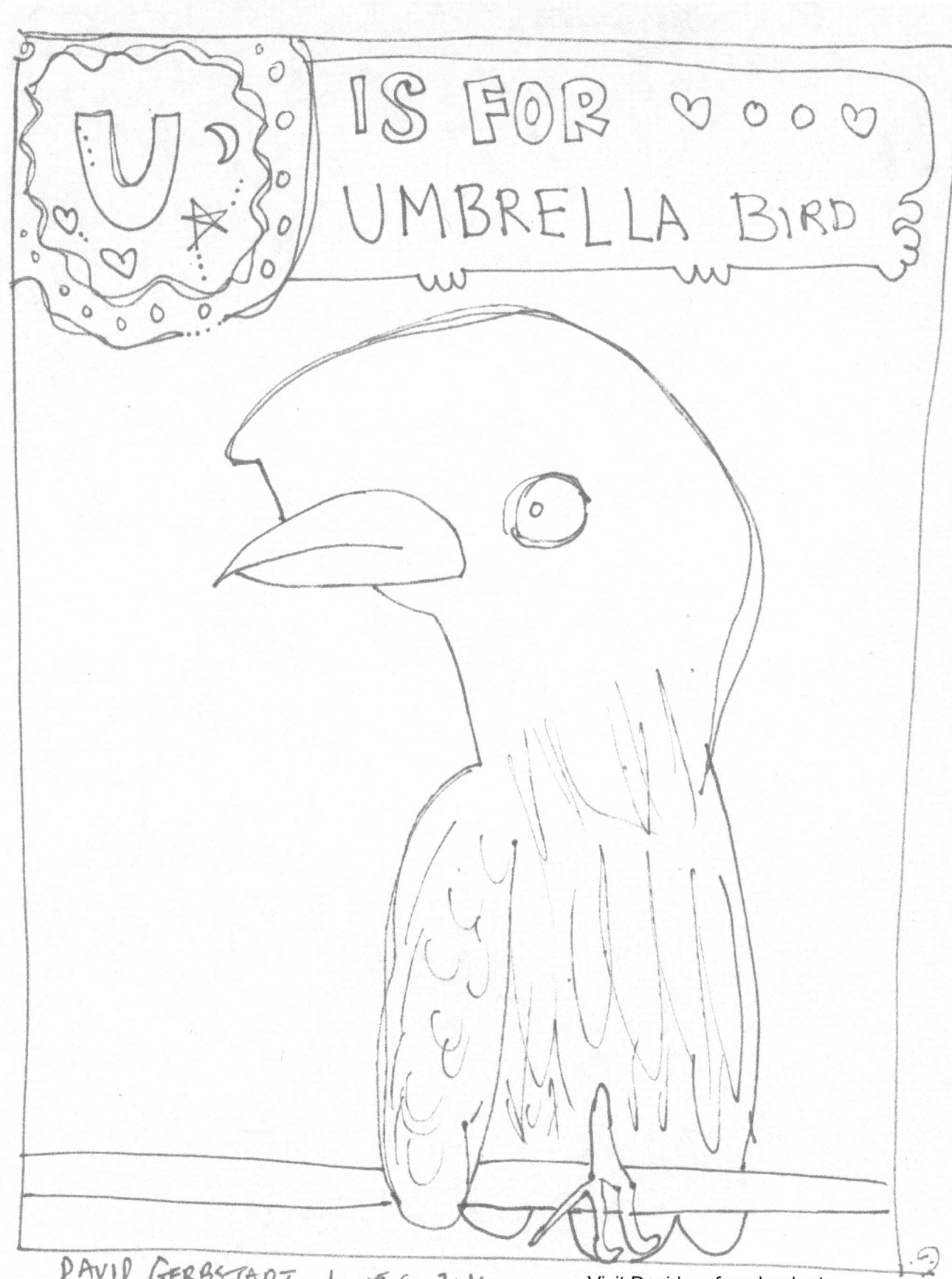

U IS FOR ♡ ∘ ∘ ∘ ♡
UMBRELLA BIRD

DAVID GERBSTADT JUNE 6. 2016.

"V" IS FOR VUL CAN...

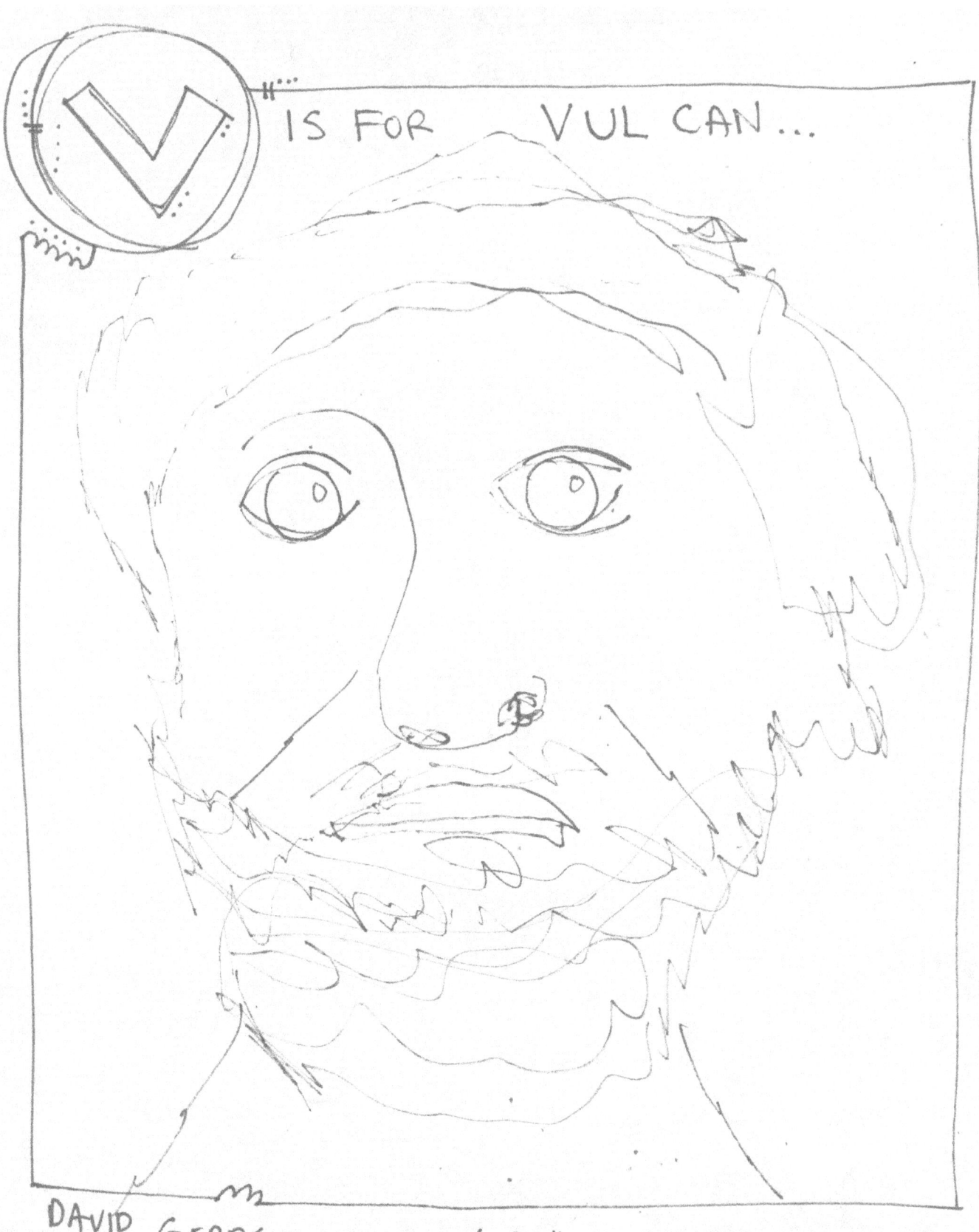

DAVID GERBSTADT JUNE 6, 2016...

Visit David on face book at:
www.facebook.com/david.gerbstadt

Coloring book and more books by
David Gerbstadt on Amazon.com

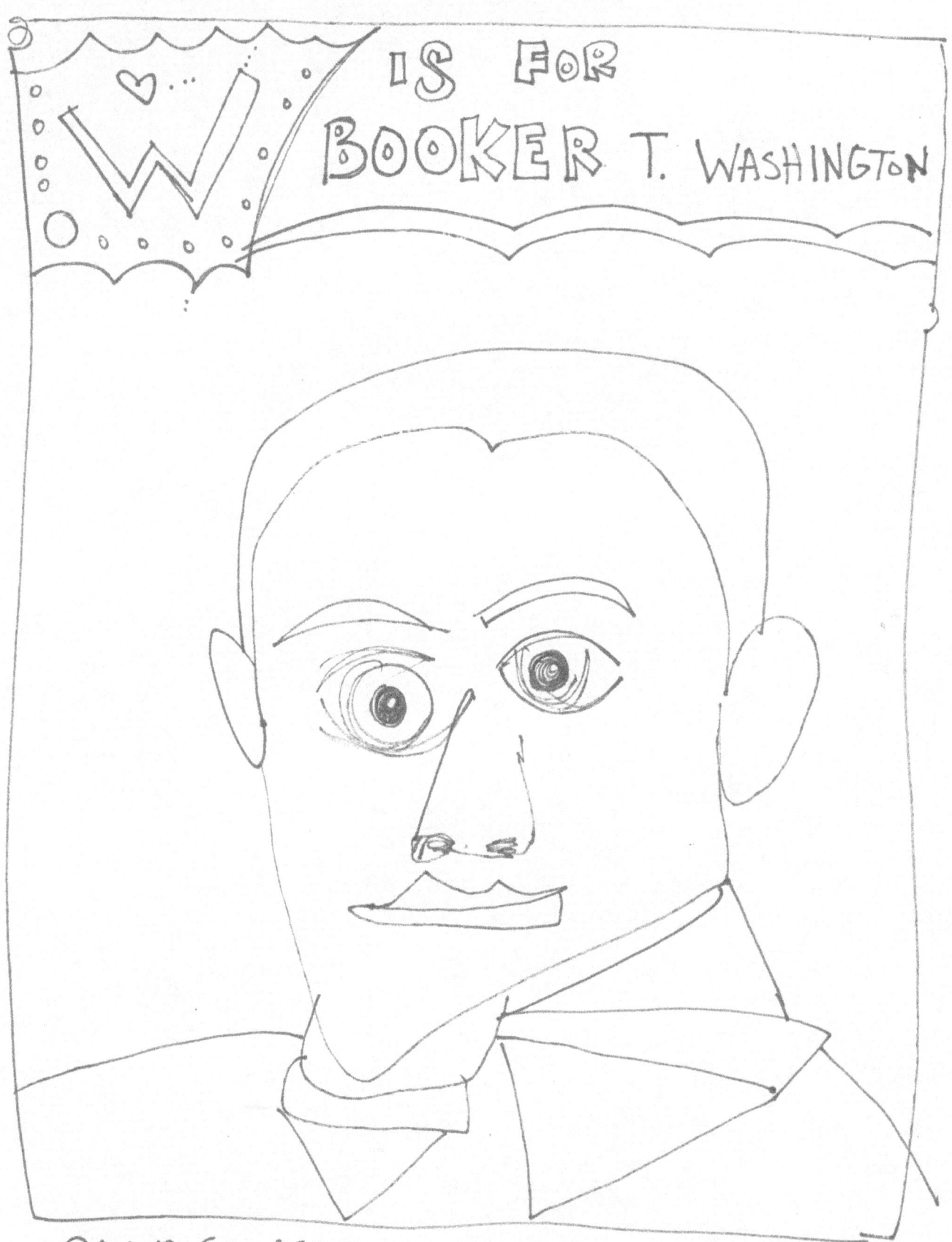

W IS FOR BOOKER T. WASHINGTON

DAVID GERBSTADT JUNE 6, 2016.

Visit David on face book at:
www.facebook.com/david.gerbstadt

Coloring book and more books by
David Gerbstadt on Amazon.com

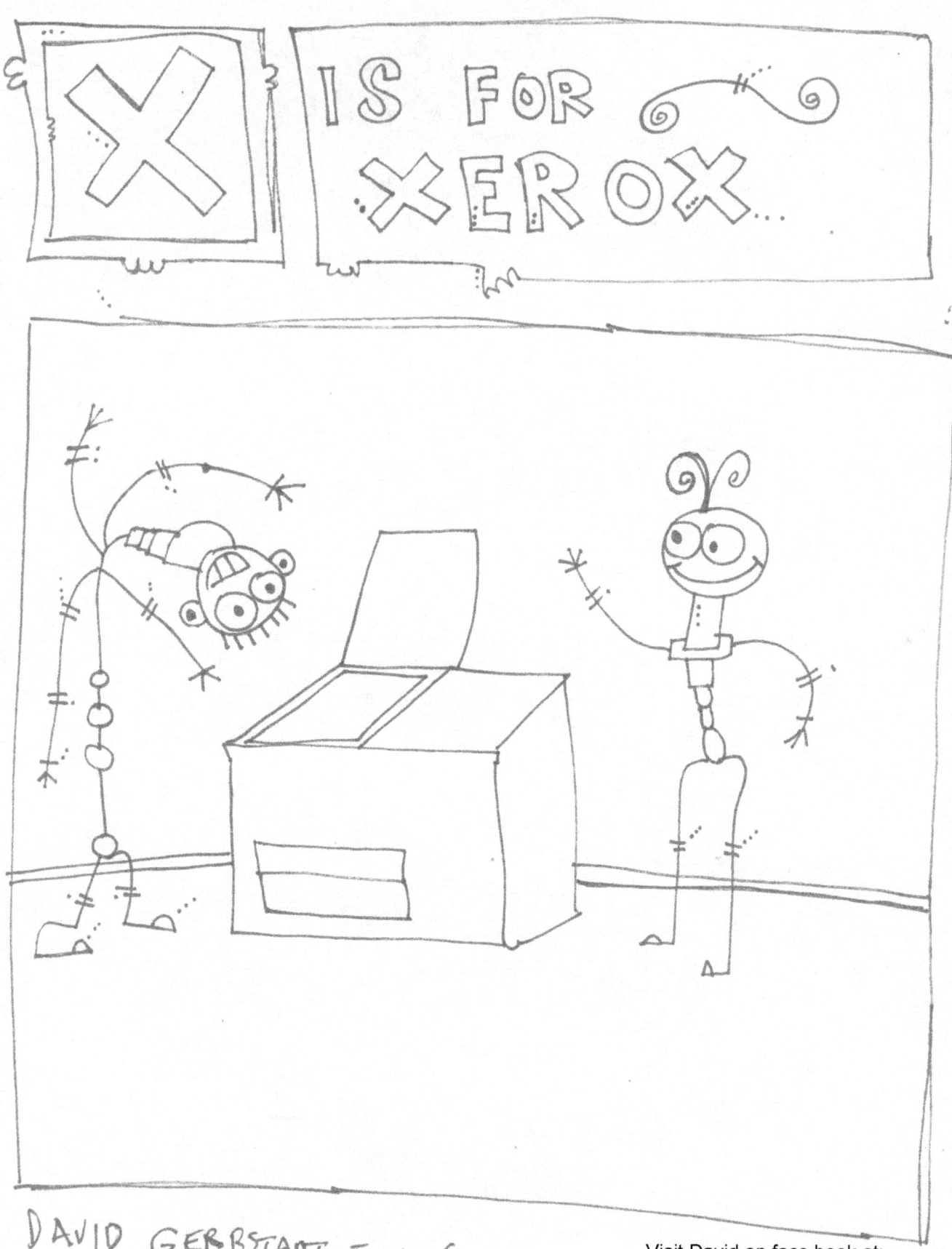

DAVID GERBSTADT JUNE 6. 2016...

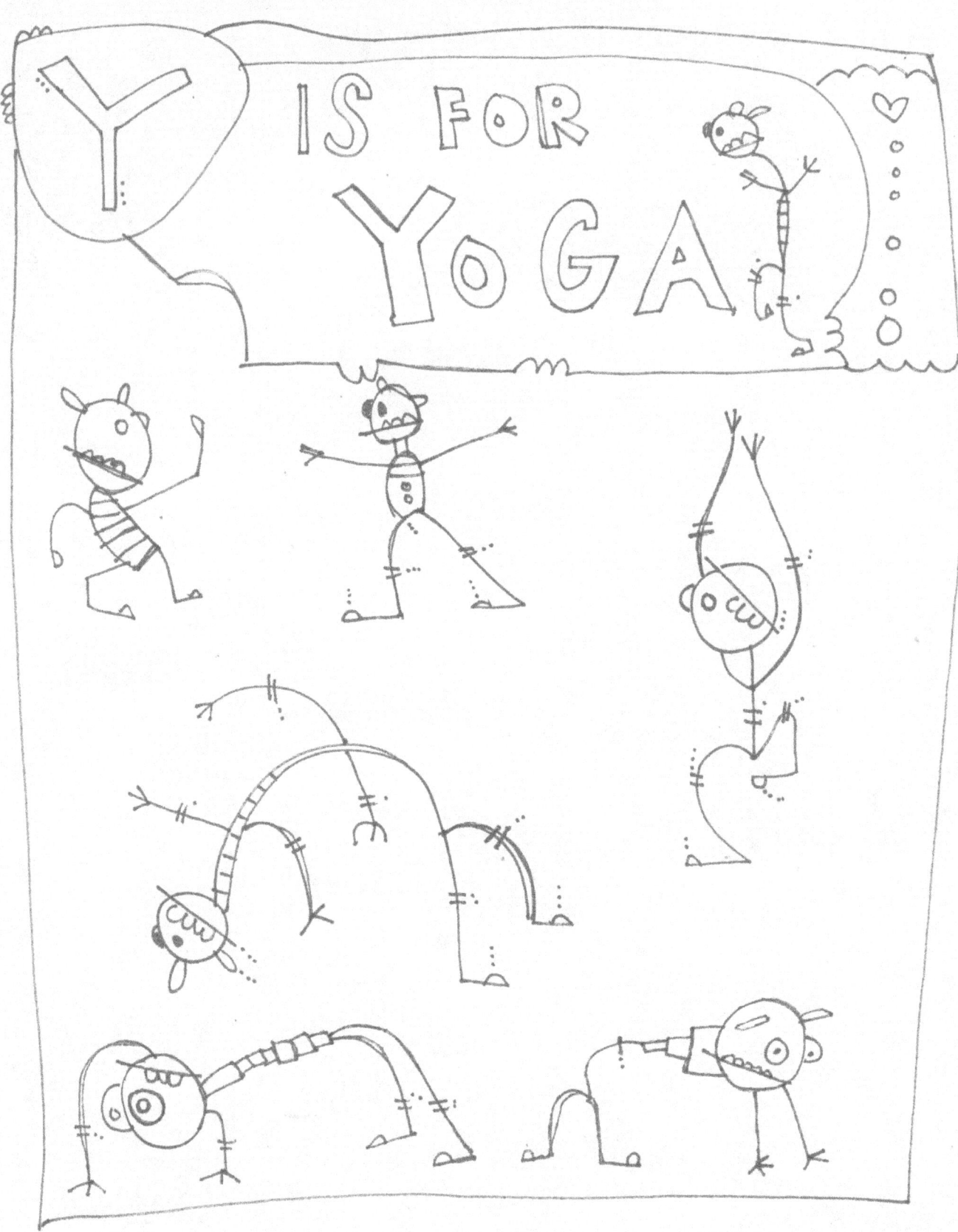

DAVID GERBSTADT JUNE 6 .2016..

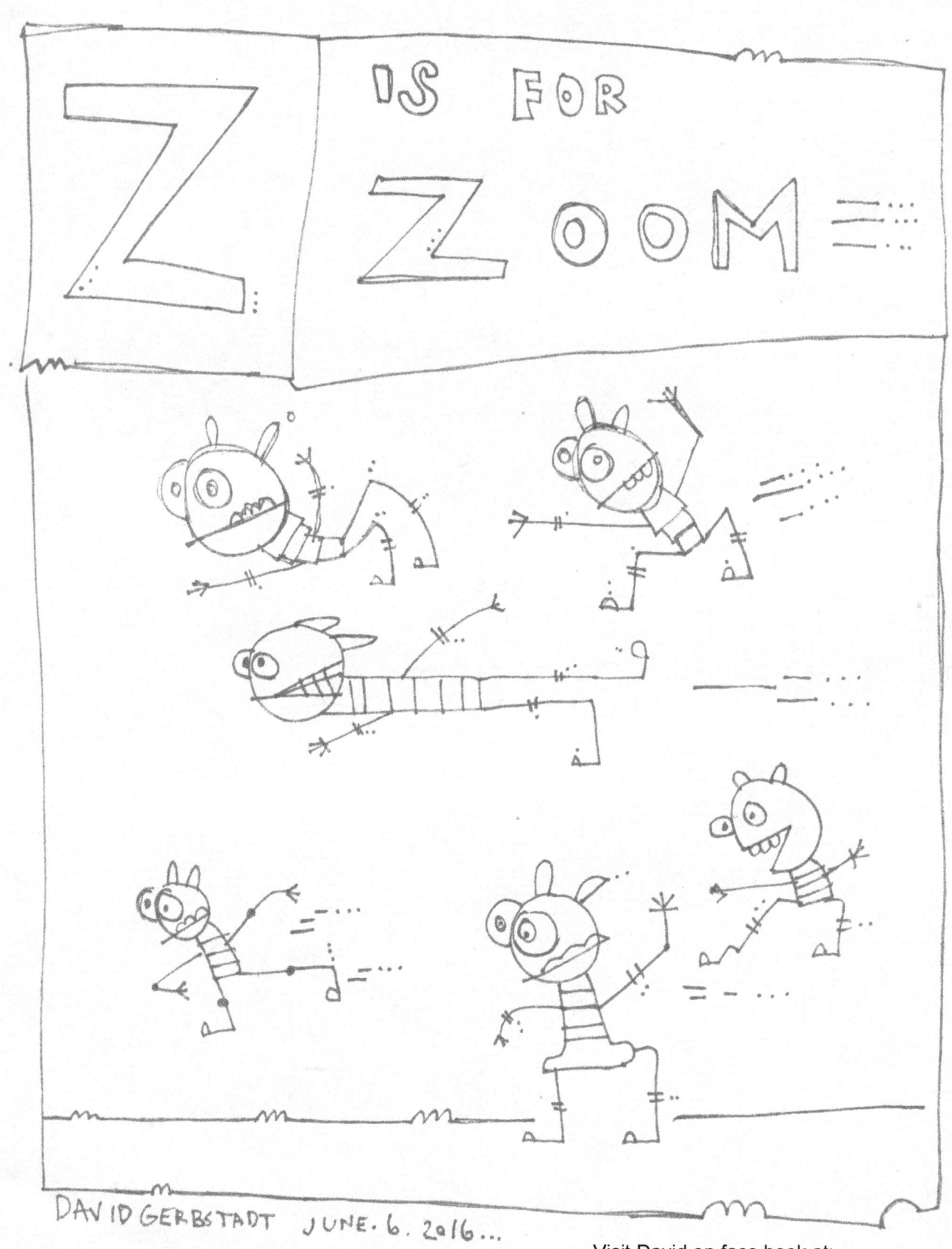

DAVID GERBSTADT JUNE. 6. 2016...

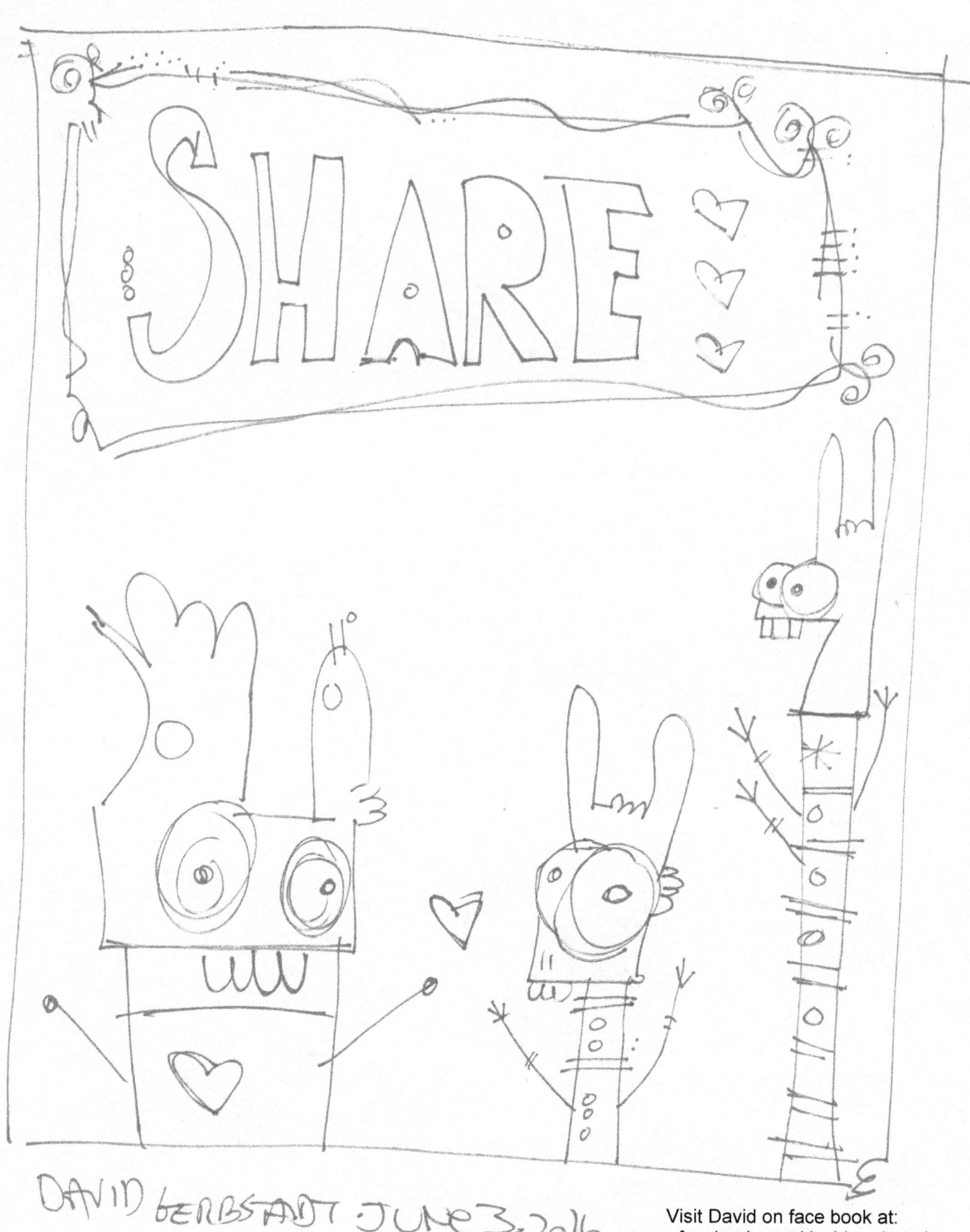

DAVID GERBSTADT · JUNE 3, 2016

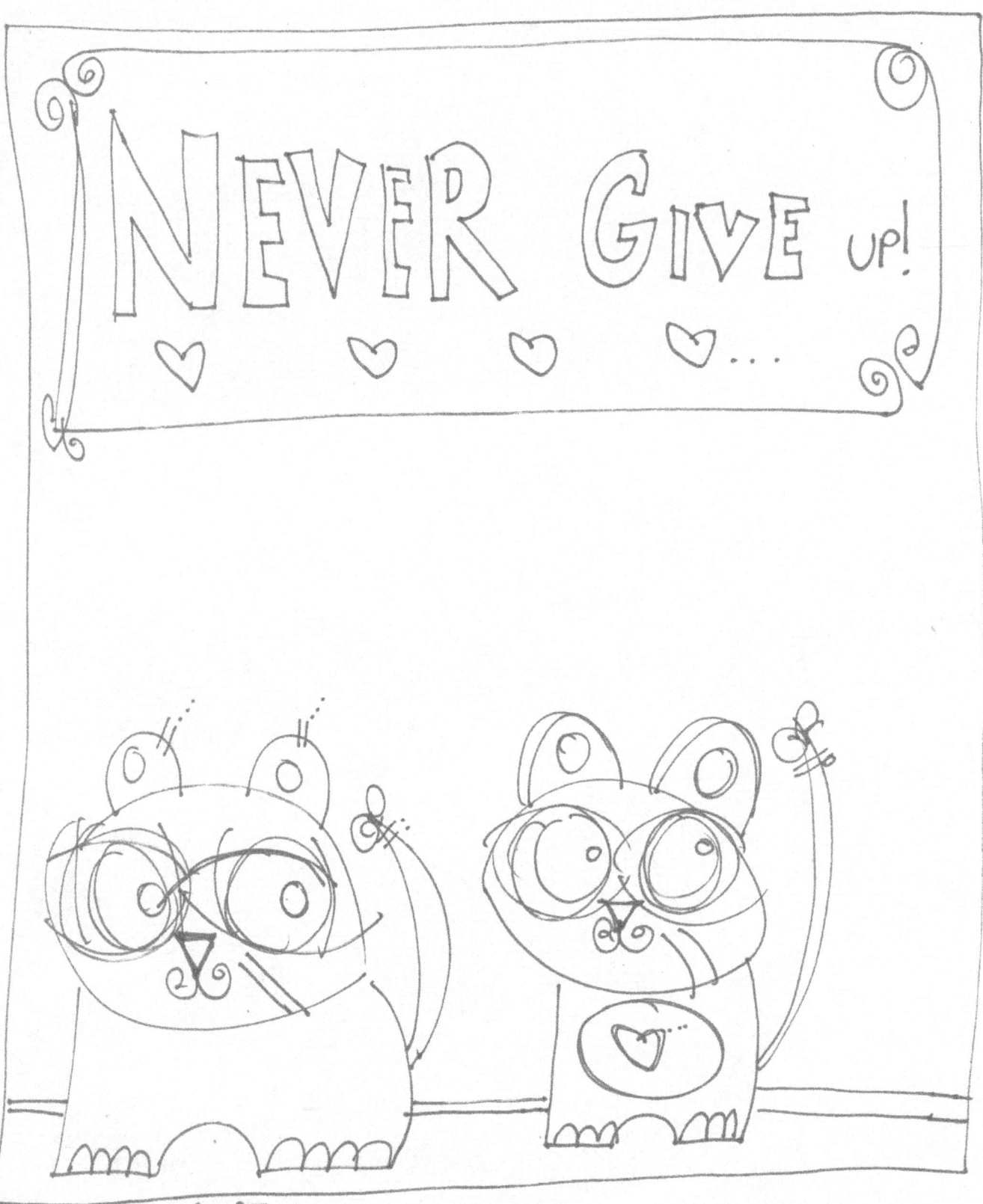

DAVID GERBSTADT

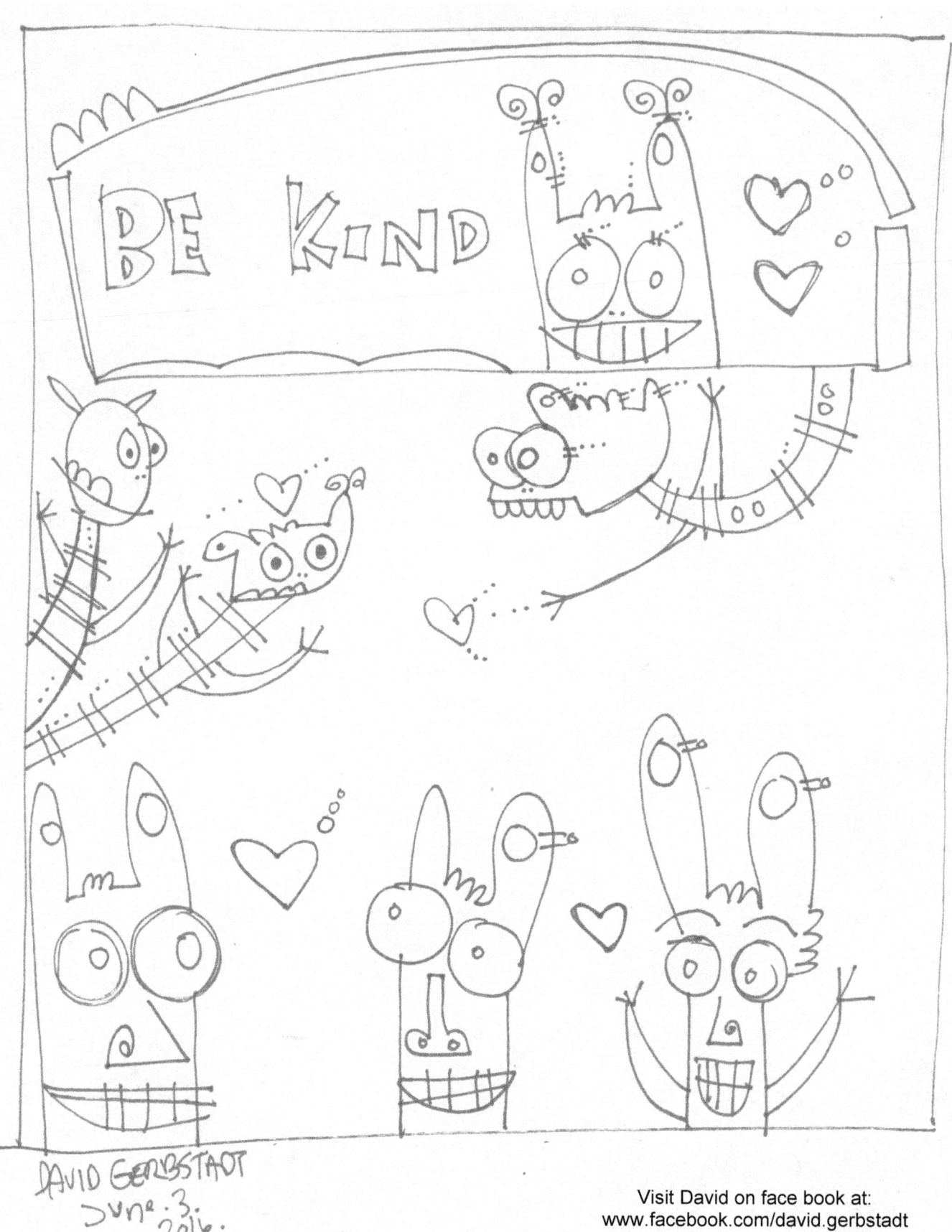

DAVID GERBSTADT
June. 3.
2016.

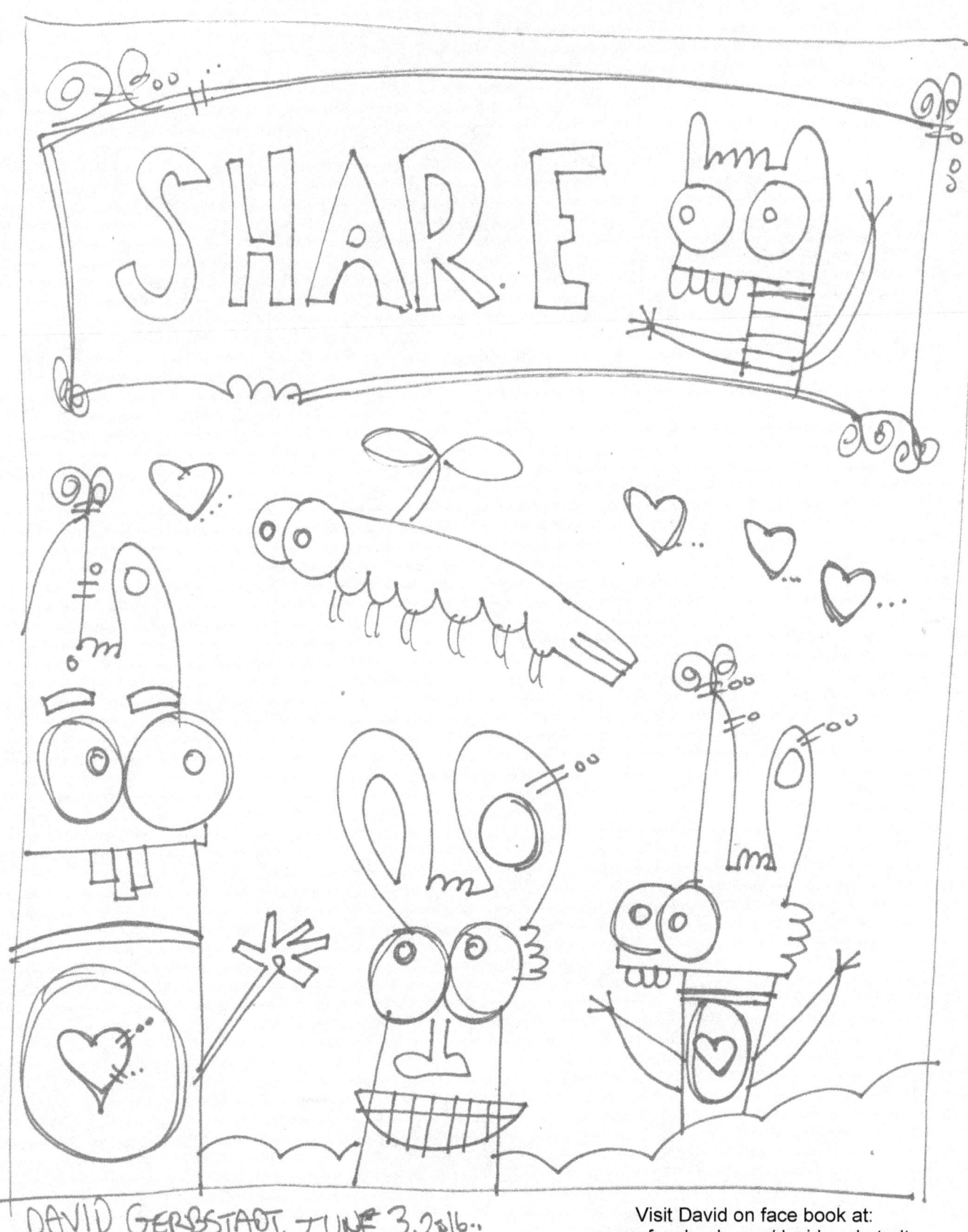

DAVID GERBSTADT JUNE 3, 2016

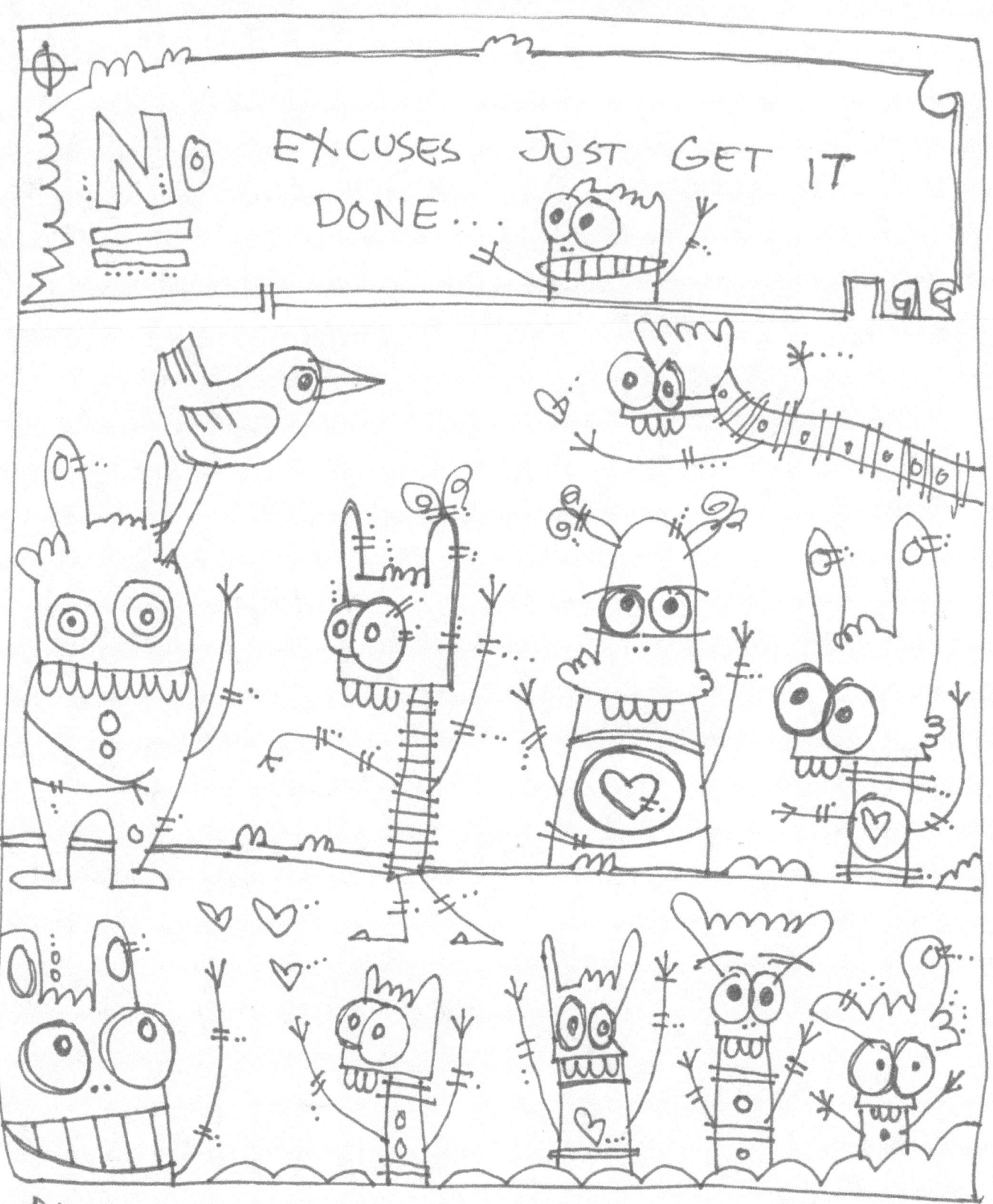

DAVID GERBSTADT JUNE 6. 2016...

Visit David on face book at:
www.facebook.com/david.gerbstadt

Coloring book and more books by
David Gerbstadt on Amazon.com

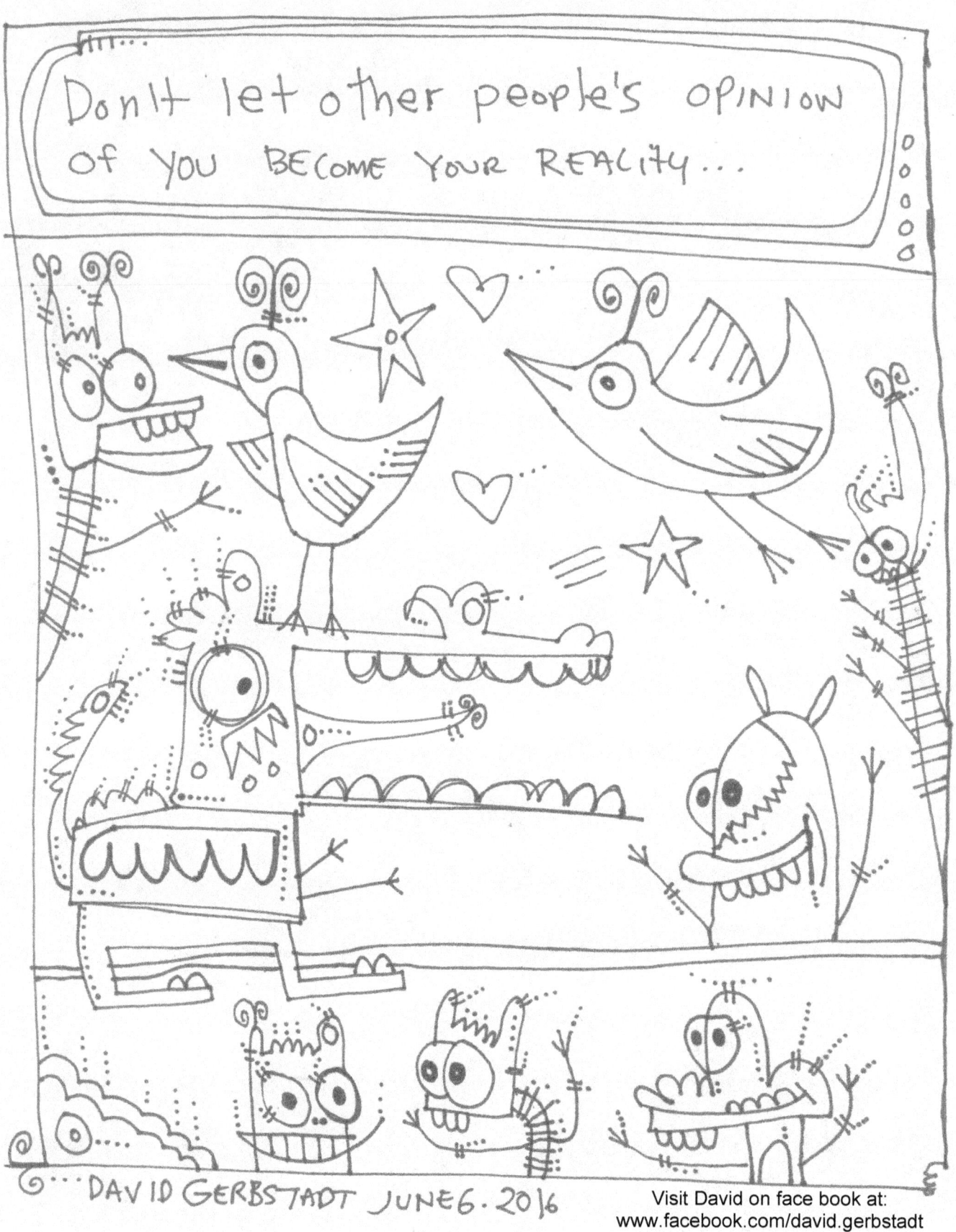

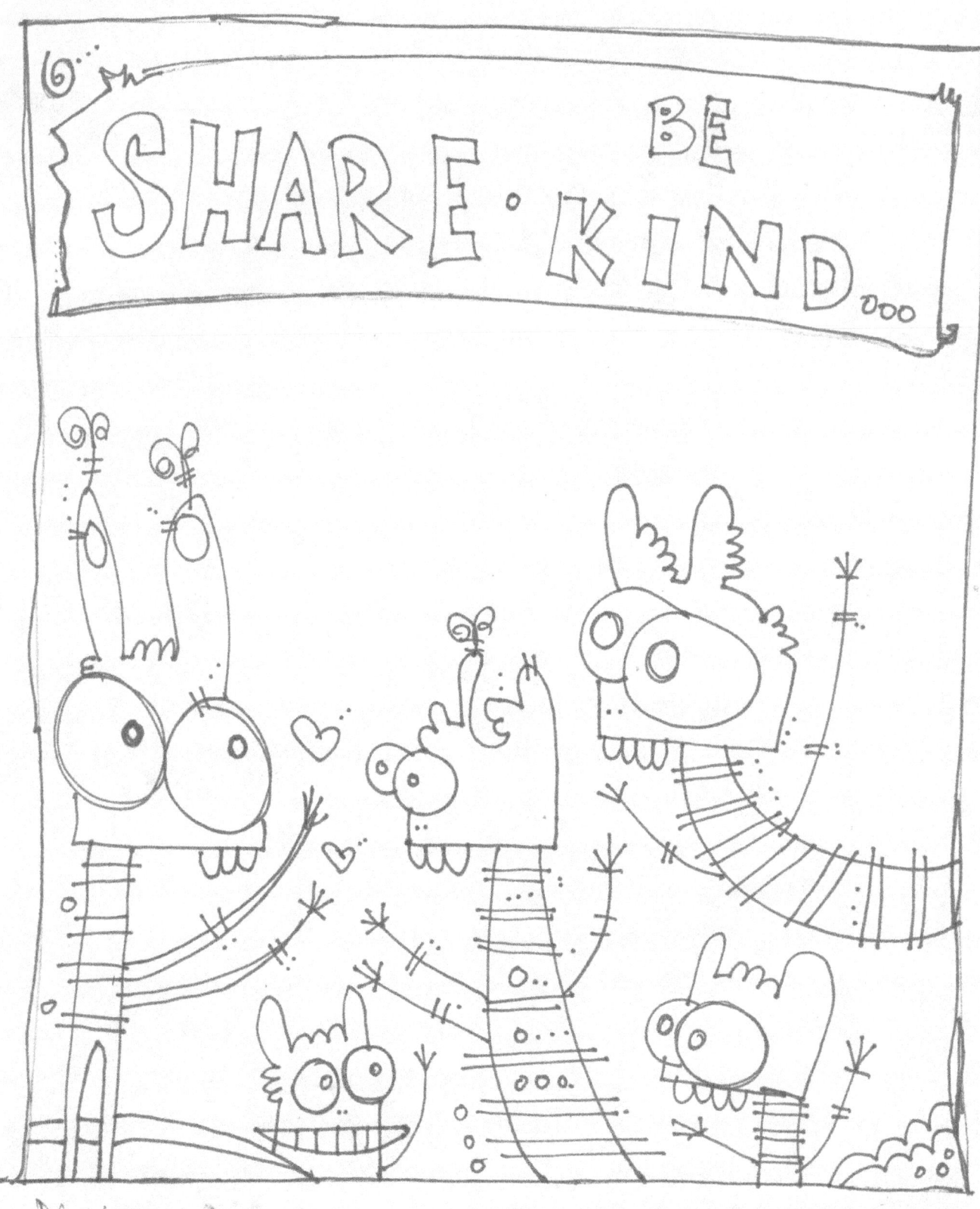

DAVID GERBSTADT JUNE 5. 2016

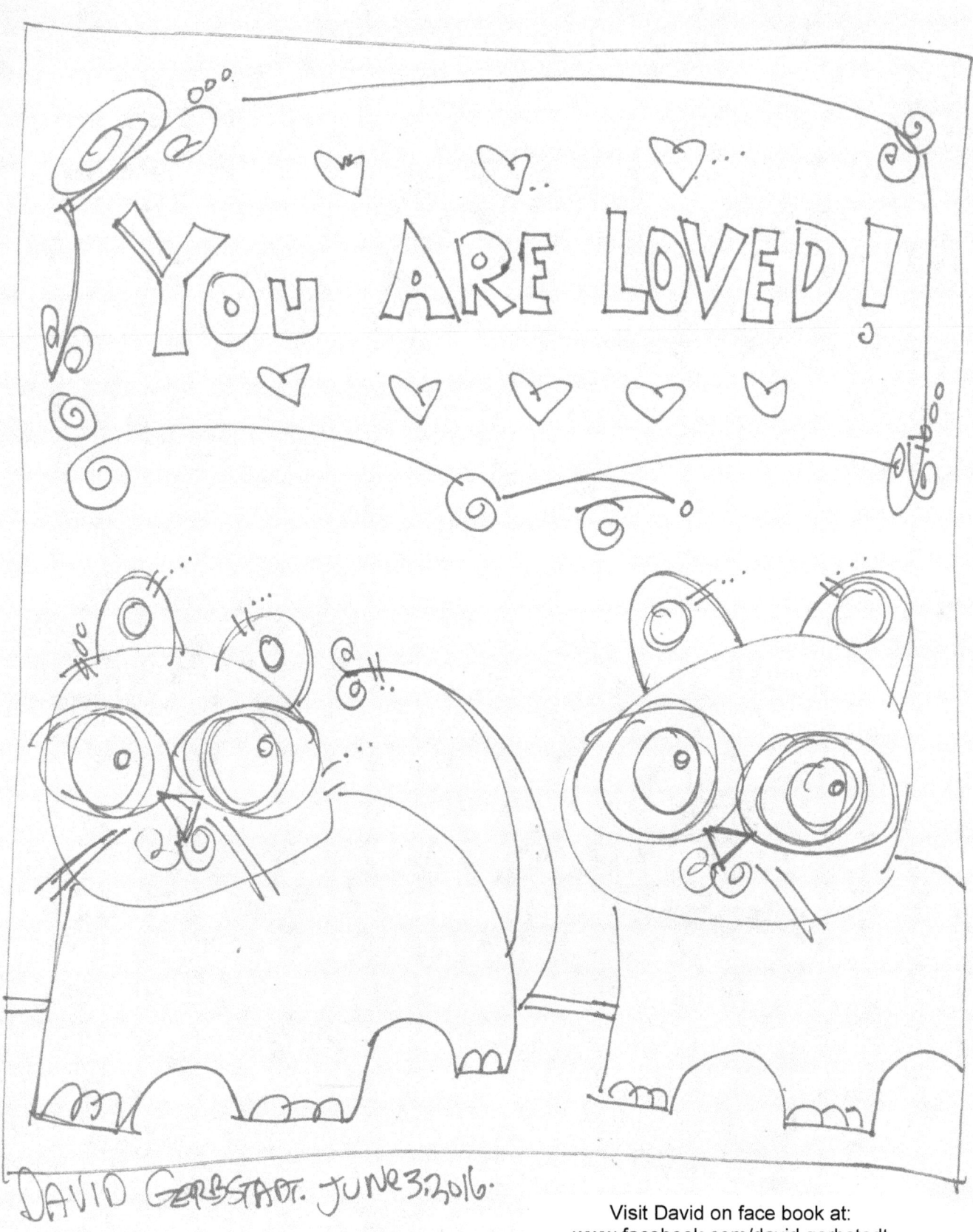

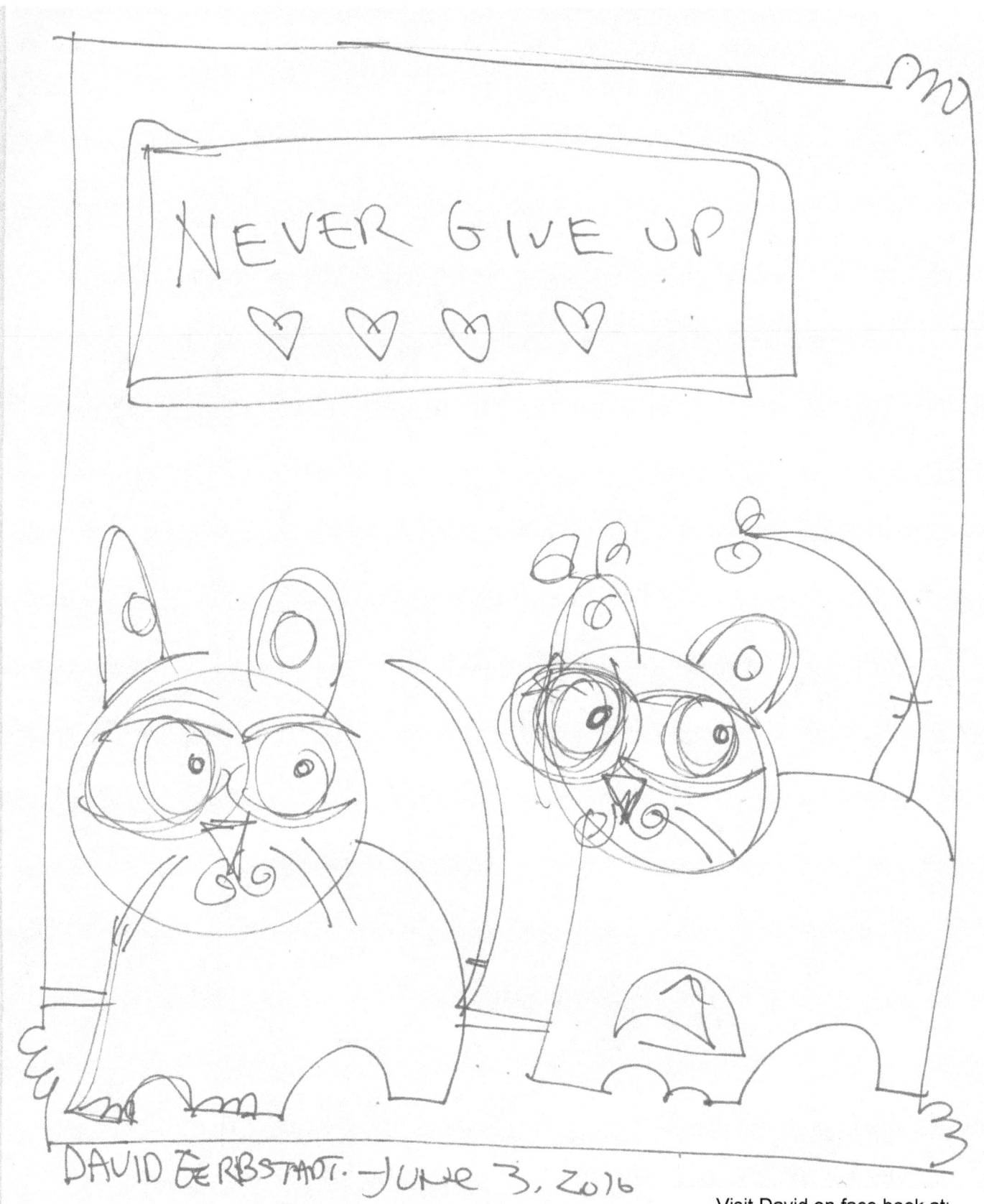

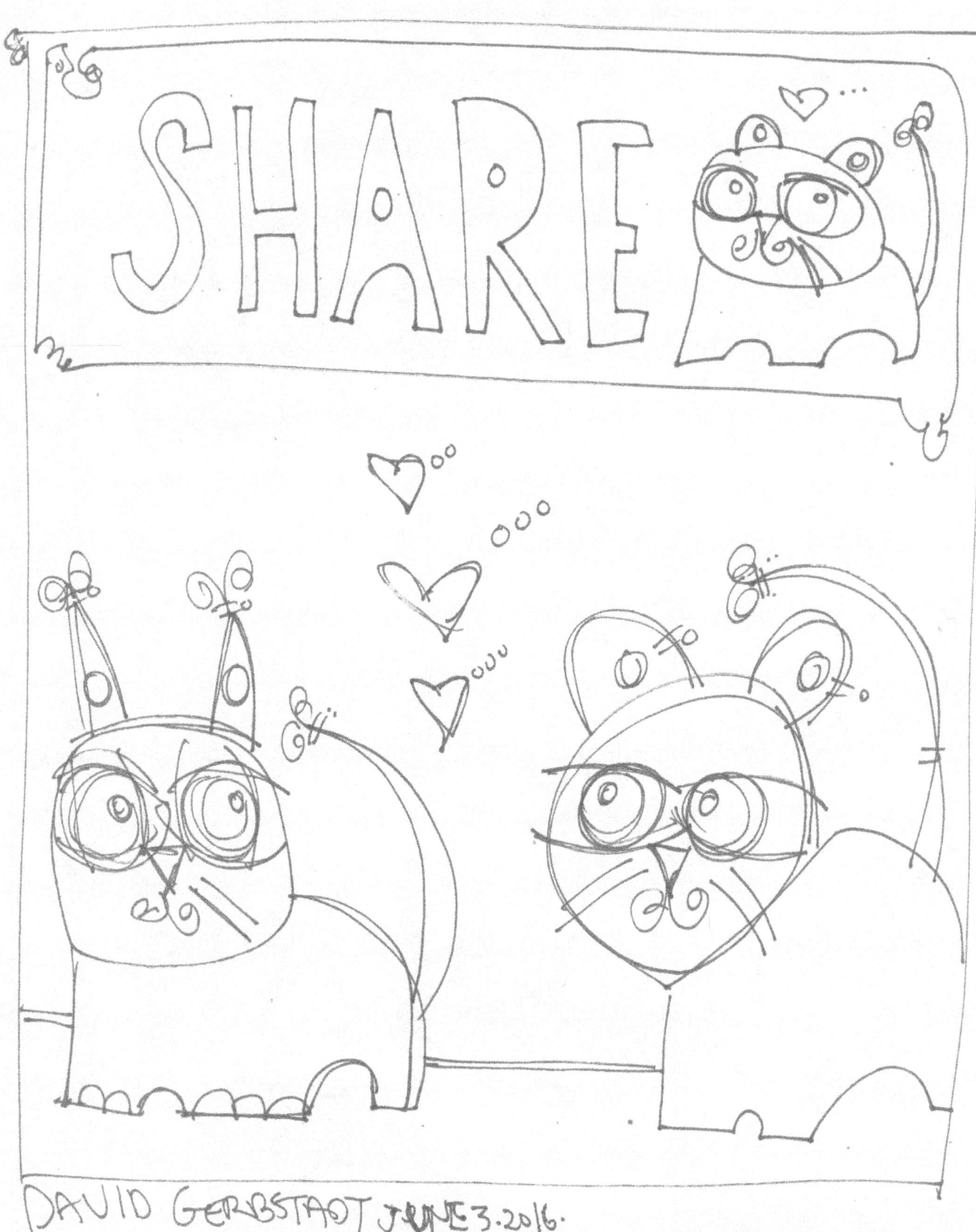

DAVID GERBSTADT JUNE 3.2016.